For two thousand years, followers of Jesus have been echoing the words of Jesus' disciples: "Lord, teach us to pray . . ." (Luke 11:1), and for two thousand years, the resurrected Christ has been responding with the familiar words of the Lord's Prayer. Deceptively simple, the prayer, as we learn to linger with it, coaxes us out into the wilds of the Spirit, where we find ourselves looking for seasoned guides who can help us negotiate the terrain. Fortunately, we have one here. Becky Harling masterfully shows us how the prayer Jesus gave us takes us into the infinite heart of our good God, transforming our lives in the process. I can't recommend this study highly enough.

ANDREW ARNDT

Pastor of New Life East; author of *Streams in the Wasteland*

For much of my adult life, I have prayed the Lord's Prayer, thinking I understood what it meant. In this unique and multilayered study of each phrase of this profound prayer, Becky Harling challenged me to go deeper, to be more honest, to fully understand forgiveness, and to explore the power of real worship. This is a Bible study that will change your life and draw you closer to your Abba Father.

CAROL KENT

Executive Director of Speak Up Ministries, speaker, and author, *He Holds My Hand: Experiencing God's Presence and Protection*

Reconnect with the Lord's Prayer and accept the invitation to fully understand its meaning. Becky Harling unpacks six invitations within the prayer. Explore this beloved prayer between Father and Son. Elevate your prayer life as you model Jesus. Break away from reciting the prayer and embrace living the prayer as a daily offering. It's a beautiful experience.

CHRISTINE ABRAHAM

Women's Ministry Director, Bible Cafe™ Ministries

Have you ever finished praying the Lord's Prayer by heart, and realized you hadn't truly embraced the rich meaning of those words? And yet, when asked how to pray, this very prayer is Jesus' response. One reason I am so delighted with author Becky Harling's newest six-week study, *Our Father*, is that it takes us through each section of the Lord's Prayer, bringing great insight and clarity. In the process, we learn not only more about our unique relationship with our Father, but how to worship, surrender, ask, forgive, and live victoriously. For years now, my husband and I have prayed this prayer together as our day begins. We cling to each familiar yet powerful word, and find fresh life and direction. Walk through six weeks of *Our Father* with friends or alone, and watch your own prayer life blossom.

LUCINDA SECREST MCDOWELL

Award-winning author of *Soul Strong* and *Life-Giving Choices*

Becky Harling's personal study *Our Father* is an emotionally resonant look at God as both the ideal of Fatherhood and Fatherhood on a personal and spiritual level. In this study, she guides the reader through navigating their own concept of fathers by sharing her own deeply affecting experiences. And then she spends the bulk of the time helping us wrestle with the question of "If God is the perfect Father, what then?" This is a very powerful and emotional book that works best when the reader, small group members, or study participants are willing to wrestle with their own hearts and relationship with God.

JAMES BROWNING

Small Group Network Development Pastor

We have memorized it. We have recited it. We have hung it on our walls, but Becky Harling's brilliant book, *Our Father*, is an invitation to LIVE the Lord's Prayer in a way that transforms our hearts, minds, and lives.

PAM FARREL

Author of 58 books, including bestselling *Men Are Like Waffles, Women Are Like Spaghetti* and *Discovering the Good News in John: A Creative Bible Study Experience*

A 6-WEEK BIBLE STUDY

OUR
FATHER

A STUDY
OF THE
LORD'S
PRAYER

BECKY HARLING

MOODY PUBLISHERS

CHICAGO

All Scripture quotations, unless otherwise indicated, are taken from the Holy Bible, New International Version®, NIV®. Copyright © 1973, 1978, 1984, 2011 by Biblica, Inc.™ Used by permission of Zondervan. All rights reserved worldwide. www.zondervan.com The "NIV" and "New International Version" are trademarks registered in the United States Patent and Trademark Office by Biblica, Inc.™

Scripture quotations marked (NLT) are taken from the Holy Bible, New Living Translation, copyright ©1996, 2004, 2015 by Tyndale House Foundation. Used by permission of Tyndale House Publishers, Carol Stream, Illinois 60188. All rights reserved.

Scripture quotations marked MSG are taken from The Message, copyright © 1993, 2002, 2018 by Eugene H. Peterson. Used by permission of NavPress. All rights reserved. Represented by Tyndale House Publishers.

All emphasis in Scripture has been added.

Names and details of some stories have been changed to protect the privacy of individuals.

Edited by Amanda Cleary Eastep
Interior design: Kaylee Dunn
Cover design: Greg Jackson / Thinkpen Design
Cover illustration of watercolor design copyright © 2022 by Alexander Evgenyevich / Shutterstock (637367359). All rights reserved.

ISBN: 978-0-8024-2967-4

Originally delivered by fleets of horse-drawn wagons, the affordable paperbacks from D. L. Moody's publishing house resourced the church and served everyday people. Now, after more than 125 years of publishing and ministry, Moody Publishers' mission remains the same—even if our delivery systems have changed a bit. For more information on other books (and resources) created from a biblical perspective, go to www.moodypublishers.com or write to:

Moody Publishers
820 N. LaSalle Boulevard
Chicago, IL 60610

1 3 5 7 9 10 8 6 4 2

Printed in the United States of America

This book is dedicated to my amazing husband,
Steve Harling.

Babe, you have truly given
our children and me a picture of our heavenly Father.
I love you!

CONTENTS

INTRODUCTION

Recently, I had the opportunity to speak at a community-wide prayer breakfast on the National Day of Prayer. I closed my message by having the audience stand and pray together. It was a powerful moment as the presence of the Lord felt palpable. Government officials, church leaders, first responders, and community advocates all prayed in unison the profound words of what we know as "The Lord's Prayer."

As I reflected on the sacredness of that event, I began to delve further into what some call "The Our Father Prayer." What I discovered is that beyond a pattern for our prayer lives, Jesus was giving us some core invitations for our discipleship journey. These principles are needed today more than ever in order to live a victorious life.

During my studying, I read an interesting article out of the diocese of Oxford. The Anglican priest recommended to people that they pray the Lord's Prayer every day.[1] I felt intrigued by this. His reasoning was that mental health issues are on the rise. The numbers of those diagnosed with anxiety, fear, depression, and suicidal ideation have risen significantly in the last few years. The priest was calling his people back and inviting them into the healing concepts of the Lord's Prayer.

In 1862, during the Civil War, a beautifully hand-scripted version of this prayer was found folded in the pocket of a fallen soldier in Corinth, Mississippi, by A. P. Green from Auburn, Indiana.[2]

I also learned that the Lord's Prayer played a key role in bringing hope amidst the tragic events of 9/11. Todd Beamer prayed the Lord's Prayer out loud on Flight 93 right before he and some fellow passengers attempted to prevent terrorists from flying the plane into Washington, DC. His actions saved the plane from hitting the Pentagon or the White House.[3] In another article about the events of 9/11, I read how a retired US Army colonel directed his coworkers, who were working in the towers when the first plane crashed, to the stairway. As he headed down the stairs, his personal pattern of saying the Lord's Prayer daily came to the surface of his mind. Mahony writes: "As I stepped into the smoky stairway, the Lord's Prayer ran through my mind; over and over and over: 'Thy will be done.' At first, I could only get through part of the prayer. But after a few floors, prayer relaxed me." Mahoney continues, "I felt God's peace, and I knew that regardless of the physical outcome, everything would be all right."[4]

Many of us grew up reciting the Lord's Prayer, yet in our recitation, we may have missed some of the deeper meaning of what Christ was teaching. Tucked within this prayer are six life-changing invitations, which, if accepted and internalized, will forever transform your life. The invitations are not simply prayer principles, they are principles of deep core discipleship. What's ironic is that though the invitations are from God, they are also petitions that we pray, inviting God into our circumstances and to change our lives. What results is a beautiful, intimate relationship with our Father.

As I have begun to dig into each invitation, my own heart has fallen more deeply in love with Jesus and become more passionate about serving Him. I have found

The Lord's Prayer

Thou to the Mercy Seat our souls doth gather,
To do our duty unto Thee .... Our Father
To whom all praise, all honor should be given,
For Thou art the Great God .... who art in heaven,
Thou, by Thy wisdom, rul'st the world's wide fame
Forever, therefore .... hallowed be Thy name.
Let nevermore delays divide us from
Thy glorious grace, but may .... Thy kingdom come.
Let Thy commands opposed be by none
Let Thy good pleasure and .... Thy will be done
And let our promptness to obey be even
The very same .... on earth, as 'tis in heaven.
Then, for our souls, O Lord, we also pray,
Thou would'st be pleased to .... Give us this day
The food of life, wherewith our souls are fed,
Sufficient raiment and .... our daily bread,
With every needful thing do Thou relieve us,
And of Thy mercy, pity .... and forgive us
All our misdeeds, for him, whom Thou didst please
To make an offering for .... our trespasses,
And, forasmuch, O Lord, as we believe
That Thou wilt pardon us .... as we forgive
Let that love teach, wherewith Thou dost acquaint us.
To pardon all .... those who trespass against us,
And, though, sometimes, Thou findst we have forgot
This love for Thee, yet help .... and lead us not
Through soul or body want, to desperation,
Nor let earth's gain drive us .... into temptation.
Let not the soul of any true believer
Fall in the time of trial .... but deliver
Yea, save them from the malice of the devil,
And, both in life and death, keep .... us from evil.
Thus pray we, Lord, for that of Thee, from whom
This may be had .... for Thine is the kingdom,
This world is of Thy work, its wond'rous story
To Thee belongs .... the power, and the glory,
And all Thy wond'rous works have ended never,
But will remain forever and .... forever.
Thus, we poor creatures would confess again,
And thus would say eternally .... Amen.

This beautiful and unique version composed in 1823, was picked up during the War of the Rebellion by A. P. Green, of Auburn, Indiana, in Corinth, Mississippi, on the morning that the Confederate forces evacuated the town, May 30, 1862. Apparently it had belonged to a soldier. The lines were printed on very heavy satin which bore the date, July 4, 1823.

myself weeping as I worship Him in complete awe; I have discovered the beauty of surrendering my will to His; I have experienced new boldness as I've asked audaciously for the needs of others as well as my own; and I have discovered more completely the freedom that comes when I forgive. Honestly, the prayer has had a profound impact on my life.

My prayer for you, dear reader, is that as you begin to study the Our Father prayer and accept the invitations offered by Jesus, you'll fall more completely in love with Jesus. Practice reading the Word of God not just for information but for life transformation. As we study, you'll come to love God as Father, you will be drawn into worship, you'll be invited to surrender your will in favor of His, you'll ask boldly for your needs to be met, you'll learn to forgive freely and discover freedom as a result, and finally, you'll learn to walk in victory!

Are you ready?

My question to you is are you willing and ready to join me? Are you willing to open the invitations that Christ offers in His prayer? Come. Let's get started as we consider that Jesus . . .

- Invites us to know God as our Father
- Invites us to worship as a lifestyle
- Invites us to surrender our will in favor of His
- Invites us to ask audaciously for what we need
- Invites us to forgive to find freedom
- Invites us to experience victory over evil

What You Can Expect

As we journey through this study together, we will look more closely at each invitation. Though you'll see a traditional version of the Our Father prayer at the end of this section—the way most of us grew up reciting it—we're going to study in the New International Version (NIV). Each day will include some homework for you. Don't let the word "homework" freak you out. Each day just offers questions for you to answer to help you understand the Our Father prayer more fully. Don't get discouraged if you fall behind. It's no big deal. You'll resonate with some days more than others. If on one day you find the Holy Spirit speaking to your heart, take a bit longer that day. There are no rules in this study. My goal is simply to have you respond to the amazing invitations that Jesus offers through His prayer.

Each day is divided into six sections:

Explore: In this section, we will look not only at the specific passage where the Lord's Prayer is found (Matt. 6:9–13), we will study each invitation offered. In addition, we'll also study correlating passages.

Reflect: After studying each invitation from different Bible passages, there will be some questions to guide personal reflection. We always want to read and study the Scriptures for life transformation, not simply for information.

Apply: In this section, you will be encouraged to answer very specifically, *What is God's invitation to me personally today?* In this way, we allow the Holy Spirit to speak to our hearts specifically through His Word.

Pray: I am a firm believer in praying Scripture. In this section, you will find a prayer written based on Scripture. Then there will be some blank space under the title: Now It's Your Turn. There you will be encouraged to write out your own prayer, using Scripture from the day's study.

Listen: Jesus invites us to make praise a priority in our lives. Each day there will be a suggested song for you to listen to in order to prompt your praise. Please note: You may not like the song I choose. No worries. Simply choose your own in its place. The important thing is that you learn to allow worship music to prompt your praise.

Memorize: When we memorize Scripture, we give the Holy Spirit a tool to use in our transformation. The more you memorize, the more the Holy Spirit will bring it to your memory when you need it.

Friend, I'm so excited for you to join me in this journey of studying the Lord's Prayer! I'm guessing you, like me, are going to fall deeper in love with Jesus because of your study. Would you take a moment before we begin to ask the Holy Spirit to use this study to transform your thinking? Ask Him to open your eyes to all He wants to show you and to awaken in your heart a deeper love for Christ!

Blessings and Prayers,

Becky

Our Father, who art in heaven,

hallowed be thy Name.

thy Kingdom come,

thy will be done

on earth as it is in heaven.

Give us this day our daily bread.

And forgive us our trespasses,

as we forgive those who trespass against us.

And lead us not into temptation,

but deliver us from evil.

For thine is the kingdom,

and the power, and the glory,

for ever and ever.

Amen.

THE INVITATION TO KNOW GOD AS FATHER

"Our Father in Heaven"

MATTHEW 6:9

RADICAL THEOLOGY

My friend Annabelle grew up in Uganda in a Muslim home. One night, her stepbrother abused her, and to her horror, Annabelle realized her father would do nothing to protect her. Things only got worse as Annabelle (only thirteen at the time) discovered there was a plan to marry her off to a teacher of Islam who was already married. Terrified, Annabelle ran away.

Annabelle described her pain with these words: "As time went by, I never trusted people. Not even my parents. I learned to cover my pain in work. I disconnected from my father. I felt he didn't want us. He didn't protect us enough. He didn't stay. I wondered if life was worth living. They say incest is a curse—I struggled with the perception that I was going to live all my life a cursed girl. Who was going to ever marry me? I hated men—and I detested the word FATHER!"

In high school, Annabelle attempted to take her own life. The pain was too great. It wasn't until Annabelle met Jesus that her life was radically changed. Annabelle and her husband, Isaac, now lead a ministry called the Remnant Generation that seeks to rescue girls from trafficking. Annabelle's husband is seeking to teach dads how to be the fathers God calls them to be.

As I travel and speak, many women have shared with me their stories of father wounds and how those hurts have left them scarred and broken. It's not just women who have suffered, but many men have also suffered. They've spoken to me about how their own father wounds have impacted their confidence as fathers. Unfortunately, the stories are all too common.

Father wounds run deep and are at the root of much of our brokenness. They are also at the root of many mental health issues. In one article I read, the author listed just a few of the ways that father wounds impact our lives: low self-esteem and low confidence, anxiety, depression, anger and rage, and either rigidity or the inability to set clear boundaries.[1] Wow!

I am no stranger to father issues. My father, though in ministry, was abusive. spiritually, emotionally, physically, and sexually. I remember well the counselor who told me I had to separate my earthly father from my heavenly Father. I'm not going to lie; it wasn't easy. I spent countless hours on my knees asking God for a new picture of Him as my Father.

As I've had the privilege of traveling and speaking around the world, I have seen and heard firsthand that thousands have trouble seeing God as a loving Father because of deep wounds from their earthly father. Maybe that's true for you as well.

When Jesus taught His disciples to pray the Lord's Prayer, He introduced rather radical theology. Almighty God, the maker of the heavens and the earth, wanted a Father-child relationship with us. I imagine the religious leaders in the crowd listening to Jesus shook their heads in disbelief. As religious rule followers, they were accustomed to teaching people to pray at certain times of the day and using very specific words: "Hear, O Israel: The Lord our God, the Lord is one" (Deut. 6:4). The prayers of the religious leaders were rote and pompous, done for show to impress their followers. They declared allegiance to the kingdom of God; however, this was more an allegiance to their own religiosity. Their prayers lacked both authenticity and warmth. Instead, they were filled with lofty theological phrases. As a result, many saw God as a distant deity concerned with people keeping all the rules.

Jesus came to reveal the truth about the Father heart of God. He wanted folks to realize they could have an intimate relationship with God. Let's dive into this theology a bit deeper. Before we get to the Lord's Prayer, we need to consider the context for Jesus' teaching. Open your Bible to Matthew 6.

EXPLORE

Before Jesus told His disciples, "This, then, is how you should pray" (Matt. 6:9), He described the prayers of the religious leaders.

READ MATTHEW 6:5-8

What phrases did Jesus use to describe how the religious leaders of the day prayed?

The Greek word for "hypocrite" that Jesus used here described a person who is playacting or reading a script.[2] Jesus is basically accusing the religious leaders of the day of playacting for the approval of people. To put it simply, the religious leaders were praying for show.

God wants to have an intimate relationship with us, but in order for that to happen, our prayers have to be vulnerable and authentic.

READ MATTHEW 6:6-8

How does Jesus describe the way we are to pray here?

Does this mean we are never to participate in corporate prayer? Why or why not?

READ MATTHEW 6:8

What does this verse teach us about our relationship with God as our Father?

REFLECT

READ MATTHEW 7:10-11

If the "stone" in this verse represents emotional coldness and the "snake" represents abuse, these could describe some of the "gifts" our earthly fathers gave us.

What do these verses teach about the Father heart of God?

Circle in your Bible the phrase in verse 11 that says "good gifts." What are some of the good gifts God the Father has given you because He loves you? List ten of those gifts in the space below:

How might your life look different if you truly believed God the Father was madly in love with you and delighted to give you good gifts?

APPLY

What is God's invitation to you personally from this passage?

PRAY

Dearest Father God, what an incredible privilege to call You Abba, *Father, just as Jesus did. Thank You for pursuing my heart and wanting an intimate relationship with me. I praise You that I can authentically bring before You every wound of my heart, and that You, as a loving Father, bend down to listen. I praise You that as I begin this study of the Our Father prayer, Your Holy Spirit will awaken my heart to love You more dearly.* (Based on Rom. 8:15; Ps. 116:2 [NLT]; Matt. 6:9.)

Now It's Your Turn

Write your prayer of praise based on Scripture in the space below:

LISTEN

"Our Father," sung by Jenn Johnson (Bethel Music)[3]

MEMORIZE

Use the translation of your choice to memorize Psalm 103:13.

ADOPTED!

Our family is passionate about adoption. In fact, one of my grandsons is adopted. I remember so well going with my daughter and her husband to meet our new grandson. Excitement and anticipation filled my heart. I remember the exact moment I laid eyes on him and held him in my arms. Oh, my! There are not adequate words! Tears clouded my eyes, and my heart completely melted. Months of prayer had led to that moment. I fell categorically, madly in love with this tiny little boy. When the adoption was finalized, we celebrated big-time as a family.

Adoption is costly. I remember all the fundraisers we had as a family to raise the money for our kids to be able to adopt. It's costly in other ways as well. Even if parents adopt through the foster care system, which is usually free, the child being adopted has experienced trauma that often plays out in the family system. Adoption is costly to the family system.

As we consider the opening of the Lord's Prayer, and specifically the phrase "Our Father," we can't ignore what our adoption cost the Father. Today, we're going to look at our adoption into God's family—after all, that's why we can call God our

Father. We're going to consider what our adoption cost not only Jesus but also Father God. Our adoption process begins at the cross. Open your Bible to Matthew 27.

EXPLORE

The older I get, the more the crucifixion of Jesus means to me. I cannot even fathom the agony of our Savior Jesus on the cross. The love that drove Him to finish the work of our adoption is mind-blowing.

READ MATTHEW 27:26-56

Using your own words, describe the crucifixion of Jesus.

Sit with the pain of the crucifixion for five silent minutes. Ask the Holy Spirit to help your mind grasp the depth of the pain. Ask Him to awaken in your heart a new appreciation for the agony Jesus suffered as He hung on the cross.

Write down the first adjectives that come to mind when you consider the horror of Jesus' death.

READ MATTHEW 27:46

What do you think Father God was feeling at this time?

Pastor and author Tim Keller, in his book *Walking with God through Pain and Suffering*, writes that Jesus . . .

> was abandoned, denied, and betrayed by all the people he had poured his life into, and on the cross he was forsaken by even his father (Matt. 27:46). This final experience, ultimately unfathomable to us, means infinite, cosmic agony beyond the knowledge of any of us on earth. For the ultimate suffering is the loss of love, and this was the loss of an eternal, perfect love. There is nothing more difficult than the disruption and loss of family relationships, but here we see that "God knows what it is like to suffer . . . because he has personally suffered in the most severe way possible . . . the agony of loss by death, the separation from a beloved, [and] the disruption of his own family (the Trinity) by the immensity of his own wrath against sin."[4]

God the Son took all the brunt of God the Father's wrath against sin for you and me. It cost the Son His life. It cost the Father the horror of watching His own beloved Son tortured and crucified for crimes He never committed. It cost the first separation of the family system of the Trinity. Ah, friend, make no mistake, the price of your adoption was beyond anything you can imagine!

READ ROMANS 8:1-8

According to this passage, for those of us who have put our faith in Christ, how do we benefit from Christ's death on the cross?

READ ROMANS 8:9-16

How does the Holy Spirit help us realize the fullness of our adoption?

READ ROMANS 8:15

Circle in your Bible the phrase "Abba, Father!" This was the most tender of all names with which children in Middle Eastern culture could address their fathers. What does this verse teach you about the type of relationship God the Father wants to have with you?

REFLECT

Today, we've studied the cost of your adoption. *What emotions has today stirred up within you? Journal about your feelings in the space below.*

After studying the cost of your adoption today, how would you describe the Father heart of God to a friend?

When you think of the Lord's Prayer, how does understanding your adoption change your understanding of the phrase "Our Father"?

APPLY

What is God's invitation to you personally today?

PRAY

Father God, that You, the God of the universe, have adopted me as Your precious child is beyond my human understanding! It staggers my mind to think about how much You love me and how much love You continue to lavish on a daily basis. I praise You and thank You that You have chosen me and adopted me. Thank You for cherishing me as Your beloved child. (Based on 1 John 3:1; Eph. 1:3–4)

Now It's Your Turn

Write out a prayer of praise to God the Father for His initiating your adoption into His family.

LISTEN

"Run to the Father," sung by Cody Carnes[5]

MEMORIZE

Write out Psalm 103:13 from memory in the space below.

THE PORTRAIT OF A LOVING FATHER

I remember so well years ago when our daughter Keri was six years old. It was during the Beanie Baby rage. Whenever Keri had extra money, she bought another of the popular plush animals filled with "beans."

One Saturday our son was in a soccer tournament, so we spent the day traipsing from field to field, and Keri brought "Stinky," her brand-new toy skunk. That night when we tucked Keri in, it dawned on her she had lost Stinky on one of the fields. If your child has ever spent their own money on a stuffed animal, you know what followed. Keri was sobbing. We prayed that Stinky would show up. (If you're a parent or grandparent you know that God is fine when we pray that lost stuffed animals would be found.) After many, *many* tears, Keri fell asleep.

The next morning, my husband, Steve, got up around 5 a.m. He went back to those soccer fields across town and spent two hours searching every field. Finally, after more than two hours, he walked in the door triumphantly with Stinky! I gotta tell you, he won Keri's heart forever!

Steve modeled the heart of the Father for our daughter. In Luke 15, Jesus gives us a poignant portrait of the loving Father heart of God. He tells three stories of lost things, culminating in the dramatic loss of a son. This is where I want to draw your attention today.

EXPLORE

READ LUKE 15:11-32

If you were to describe the father in this story to a friend, how would you describe him?

According to Dr. Kenneth Bailey, Middle Eastern fathers would never have behaved like the father in this story. By granting the request of the son, the father did what no village father would do.[6] The parable would have been shocking to listeners. According to Jewish law, a child that wasted the family's inheritance would have been shunned and possibly stoned when they tried to reenter. The father in the story Jesus told, rather than standing back with arms crossed and anger portrayed on his face, is scanning the horizon searching for his son. When the father sees his son, he gathers his robe up, exposing his ankles in a way that would be very undignified. The father runs to his son, sparing him from the village boys who would have lined the path leading into the village ready to throw stones. He hugs his son in a tight embrace, showering him with affection. He clothes his son with his very own robe and puts his ring on his son's finger!

Whenever, I teach this part of the story, I choke up! It triggers within me such a deep love for God as my Father. Ah, it is such a remarkable portrait of the love Father God has for us.

In the story, what do you think is the significance of the father clothing his son with his robe?

What do you think is the significance of the father giving his son his ring?

READ PSALM 103:13

How does the father in Jesus' story illustrate how the psalmist describes God?

When the younger son first returns home, he wants to come home as a servant to work for his father. The father, however, wants him to come home as his child.

What is the difference between viewing your relationship with God as a servant versus as a child? List the differences below:

SERVANT	CHILD

REFLECT

You may not have had an abusive father, but every human father is imperfect.

How is the father in the story different from your earthly father?

How were you disciplined as a child?

How would you describe God the Father's heart in the realm of discipline?

How does the story of the prodigal help you trust God as your Father?

Can you think of an example from your own childhood in which someone modeled for you the Father heart of God? Write about that in the space below.

APPLY

What is God's invitation to you from this passage?

PRAY

Oh, Lord Jesus, thank You for showing me the Father heart of God. I praise You, Father God, that You are my holy, true Father whose every intention toward me is good. Thank You that You never stop pursuing me. I praise You that as I spend time with You and continually come back to You for more love, Your Holy Spirit will heal any wounds from my earthly father. I praise You that Your plans for me are good and not evil. Every trauma that I have ever faced in my life, You are able to turn around for good according to Your precious will. (Based on Luke 15:11–32; Jer. 29:11; Rom. 8:28.)

Now It's Your Turn

In the space below write out a prayer to God as your loving Father and the one who heals you from all your earthly father wounds.

LISTEN

"How Good Is He" sung by Andi Rozier (Vertical Worship)[7]

MEMORIZE

Psalm 103:13

THE RELATIONSHIPS HE DESIRES WE HAVE WITH ONE ANOTHER

Remember, the Lord's Prayer is about more than simply a "how to" for our prayer lives. It is a model not only for our prayer lives; it addresses core discipleship issues. One of those issues is unity.

Jesus chose His words intentionally. It's so interesting to me that He began His model of prayer with the pronoun "our." "Our Father." He didn't start with "my Father." Here in the West, we are often ruggedly individualistic, and we tend to make salvation a personalized thing. We fail to understand that our salvation has much broader implications than just our free ticket to heaven. When we are adopted into God's family, we become part of the family, and as such, we have a responsibility to the rest of the body of Christ.

In the context in which Jesus taught, His listeners likely had a far better understanding of this. Middle Eastern culture was built around a clan system. You were born to a family, but also born into a "clan." Often grandparents, aunts, uncles, cousins, and even second cousins made up a clan. When we are adopted into God's family, we are included into the extended family of God. Unity within the family is a big deal to Jesus.

Hours before Jesus would be crucified, one of the greatest issues on His heart was that of unity in the body. Let's take a look.

EXPLORE

READ JOHN 17

Note the context. Jesus is praying in the garden of Gethsemane as He looks to the cross. He prays:

- That the Father would be glorified (John 17:1–5)
- That His disciples would be sanctified and transformed (John 17:6–19)
- That His followers—the church—would be unified (John 17:11, 20–26)

Take a look at John 17:11. Circle the words "protect them . . . so that they may be one" in your Bible. It seems that one of Satan's greatest tactics against the church today is dividing believers.

As you consider division in the church, what are some of the issues that you see dividing believers today? List those issues below.

Jesus prayed even for those of us who would follow Him years after He ascended, that we would be one. It's astounding! He prayed that we would be one as the Trinity is one. Think about that: Father, Son, and Holy Spirit all work together in sync toward one plan and purpose. That's the measure of unity that Jesus prayed for us.

When Jesus taught His disciples to pray beginning with the phrase "Our Father," He was sending a clear message: we are to be one.

READ GALATIANS 3:26-29

Write out verse 28 in the space below.

Paul was echoing the heart of Jesus, reminding the Galatians that regardless of race, color, gender, political persuasion, or economic status, we are all one in Christ. Wow! What a reminder for this generation that feels so divided over race, political persuasion, denominational differences, and a host of other issues. Friends, we are one. As a pastor in our area likes to remind his congregation, "When we come to the table of the Lord, we don't come as male or female, we don't come as Republican or Democrat, we don't come as black or white, we come as one bride of Christ."

REFLECT

We've studied the Father heart of God this week and our adoption into a larger family. Today, we've looked at Jesus' heart for His family, which in a word is "unity." Take a deep look at your own life and ask the Holy Spirit to search you.

In what areas do you have difficulty feeling unified with those who hold different opinions from you?

Throughout the New Testament, we are commanded to love one another. *What do you think is the connection between experiencing the love of Father God and loving one another in the family of Christ?*

In what ways can you help build up other believers and assist in bringing unity in your church, community, nation, and even globally?

APPLY

What is God's invitation to you personally from today's lesson?

Oh Father God, thank You that I am part of Your family. I love You and worship You. Thank You that I now have deep belonging in Your family. Help me to take that privilege seriously. I ask that You would make me an instrument of unity within Your body. I pray that You would bring my heart into perfect union with Yours and that You would fill me with overflowing love for others. Help me weep with those who weep and rejoice with those who rejoice so that each member feels included in Your love. (Based on Eph. 2:19–22; 1 Cor. 12:26.)

Now It's Your Turn

Write out a prayer asking the Holy Spirit to give you a deeper heart of love for other believers, particularly those whom you feel are hard to love. Ask Him to use you as an instrument of unity in your church and community.

LISTEN

"Forever & Amen," sung by Cody Carnes and Kari Jobe[8]

MEMORIZE

Write out Psalm 103:13 from memory in the space below.

WEEK 1 | DAY 5

THE SECURITY AND SOLIDARITY THAT COMES FROM BELONGING TO A FAMILY

President Hebert Hoover often used the phrase "rugged individualism" to describe Americans. We value our independence and autonomy. However, this rugged individualism can be a problem, particularly in the church, because the truth is that God created us for community and connection. We were never meant to live our Christian life in isolation. From the very beginning, God's intent was for us to live in community. We see this way back in the book of Genesis, where God said, "It is not good for the man to be alone" (Gen. 2:18).

Unfortunately, within evangelical circles, we have so emphasized the "personal side" of our salvation that we have at times lived disconnected lives. When Jesus began His prayer with "Our Father," He was reminding us that beyond our personal salvation, we are invited into transformation with others. We were never intended to walk out our Christian walk alone. We are given a sense of belonging in the family of God. But as in every family, we are given both privileges and responsibilities within the family system. We need connection and relationships not only with believers from our own culture but with believers from other global cultures.

EXPLORE

Read Matthew 6:9 out loud. As you think about the Father heart of God, what do you think His desire is for His family?

Look up the following verses and write your reflections on each one:

1 JOHN 3:1–2

EPHESIANS 2:19–22

ROMANS 12:5

READ 1 CORINTHIANS 12:12–26, AND THEN ANSWER THE FOLLOWING QUESTIONS:

What does this passage teach about the body of Christ providing a sense of belonging to its members?

What does this passage teach about unity within the body of Christ?

How does this passage show the importance of each member of the body?

In light of these verses, how should we treat one another within the body of Christ?

READ GALATIANS 6:2

What does this verse teach as far as vulnerability in true community?

REFLECT

As you think about being part of the larger family of Christ, how important is authentic community within the body?

If people hold different theological views within the body of Christ, do you think it's possible to have unity? Why or why not?

How important do you think it is to Jesus that His body be unified?

As you reflect on your community, do you find it easy or hard to be authentic and vulnerable?

APPLY

What is God's invitation to you today?

PRAY

Lord Jesus, I worship You. It is so staggering to me that on the night before You were betrayed the issue that was so on Your heart was unity within the body. Oh Lord, forgive me for every time I have contributed to divisiveness or disunity within the body. I praise You that as I confess my sins, You are faithful and just to forgive me of my sins and wash me with Your blood so that I stand clean before You. I pray now, Holy Spirit, that You would give me Your heart and that the fruit of the Spirit would be evident in my life as I seek to love others. Thank You that people from every nation, tribe, and tongue will stand worshiping You before Your throne. (Based on John 17:20–23; 1 John 1:9; Gal. 5:22–23; Rev. 7:9.)

Now It's Your Turn

Write out a prayer to the Lord for the broader body of Christ. Include believers who are being persecuted for their faith and those whom you have never met but who worship Jesus Christ around the world.

LISTEN

"Always There," sung by Natalie Grant (The Belonging Co)[9]

MEMORIZE

Write out Psalm 103:13 from memory in the space below.

THE INVITATION TO WORSHIP

"Hallowed Be Your Name"

MATTHEW 6:9

GOD'S AMAZING INVITATION TO WORSHIP HIM

In the stream of Christianity in which I grew up, we were taught reverence for God's name. When my friends would flippantly use God's name in casual expressions, I would inwardly cringe. God's name is holy and deserves reverence. However, when Jesus taught us to pray, "Hallowed be your name" (Matt. 6:9), He was inviting us to go beyond just reverencing God's name to living a life of worship.

I don't know what comes to mind when you think of God inviting you to worship Him. You might think, "Well, that's what I do on Sunday morning." Or you might cringe in fear imagining God as some angry being in the sky demanding that you fall on your knees before Him. Or perhaps you wonder, "Why did God tell us to worship Him in the first place? Is God insecure that He needs us to tell Him how great He is all the time?"

When God invites us to worship, we become like what or who we worship. In other words, when we worship, we are transformed. Therefore, it's important that we place our affection and adoration on the right person (Ps. 115:8). When God invites us to worship Him and the glory of His name, He is inviting us to be transformed into His image. As we worship God and ask Him to glorify Himself through us, we are transformed.

My pastor, Andrew Arndt, describes how he was transformed when he began valuing worship.

> When I became an adolescent, I learned to love and value what happened when the people of God gathered for worship and prayer. For my part, I started to appreciate the ways in which my own humanity was powerfully provoked to *go right* when we together turned our gaze to God. I would wander in with some bizarre attitude or confusion of soul and find that, as I *faced God*, something happened to me. I would experience what Paul talked about when he said that "we all, who with unveiled faces contemplate the Lord's glory, are being transformed into his likeness with ever-increasing glory, which comes from the Lord, who is the Spirit" (2 Cor. 3:18). Something about intentionally turning my awareness to God with His people restored me, and I learned to love the encounter. I started to see it as central to everything, carrying that impulse toward worship deep into my own personal life. I craved the personal encounter with the Lord who transforms. I still do. As time has gone on, I have come to understand worship as the sort of "nuclear core" of everything else that happens for the people of God, both individually and corporately.[1]

Worship brings a sense of wholeness to our lives. When we worship in spirit and truth, our lives are brought into perfect union with Christ and we return to God's original design for our lives. Theologian N. T. Wright wrote, "Christian worship ought to bring together the often disjointed aspects of our human life. A further threefold division: Christian worship integrates the whole person, the whole community, and the whole creation."[2]

Before we go any further, pause and consider, "What exactly is worship?" Here's the definition we're going to use this week:

Worship is glorifying God

through the following actions:

Lifting our praise

Expressing our thanks

Verbalizing our love

Bowing our will[3]

What does it mean to glorify God? When we glorify something, we honor, praise, adore, or exalt. Author John Piper describes it this way: "'Glorifying' means feeling and thinking and acting in ways that reflect his greatness, that make much of God, that give evidence of the supreme greatness of all his attributes and the-all satisfying beauty of his manifold perfections."[4] God designed us to reflect His glory to the world. This is why the call to worship is not just a Sunday morning thing that we do depending on how good the band is or how well we resonate with the music.

We are to live a life of worship. We are to worship and glorify His name both in our words and actions.

Through this week, we're going to look at Jesus' invitation to us to worship Him.

EXPLORE

READ MATTHEW 6:9

Circle the word "hallowed" in your Bible.

The Greek word for "hallowed" is *hagiazó*. It means "to make holy, consecrate, sanctify . . . to declare sacred."[5] When Jesus said, "Hallowed be your name," He was inviting us to worship and show reverence, not just for God's holy name but for God Himself as the Holy One. God's names describe His character. He is as His name. Jesus isn't only saying worship God's name, He is saying worship God Himself.

READ PSALM 29:2 AND PSALM 96:9

The psalmist echoes Jesus' invitation when he writes that we are to ascribe or give God the glory due His name. Again, in Psalm 96:9, the psalmist instructs us to worship the Lord in the beauty of His holiness.

Holiness can feel so ethereal. Here's the way I would describe God's holiness: God is set apart from sin and has complete integrity and is honorable in every way. Not only is He completely separate from anything that is sinful, but He is completely dedicated to His own honor.

Let's take a deeper look at what it looks like to worship the Lord in the beauty of His holiness through the prophet Isaiah.

READ ISAIAH 6:1-8

Describe Isaiah's encounter with the Lord.

In Isaiah's vision, he saw and heard the seraphim surrounding the throne and exclaiming, "Holy, holy, holy is the LORD Almighty!" (Isa. 6:3). I don't think this was quiet chanting. I think it was loud and vibrant worship with all of heaven reverberating with the chorus of "Holy, holy, holy!" It was so vibrant that Isaiah writes that at the thunderous sound the doorposts and thresholds shook! (Isa. 6:4).

Jesus, before He came to earth incarnate, would have experienced this thunderous echo of holiness around the throne of God. I imagine Jesus had that image and the sounds in His mind as He invited us to worship the Lord using the words "Hallowed be your name"!

What was Isaiah's response to the holiness of God?

How might a fresh awakening to God's holiness help you at this season of your life?

The apostle John paints a similar picture in Revelation 4:8, which demonstrates that Isaiah's vision was a true picture of what is happening in heaven around the throne of God.

READ REVELATION 4:8-11

What is the response of the twenty-four elders? How is their response similar to that of Isaiah?

The Greek word for "worship" used in Revelation 4:10 is *proskuneó*, meaning "to prostrate oneself, bow down in obedience, show reverence, do homage, worship and adore."[6] The word "worship" gives us a true picture for what Christ was talking about when He said, "Hallowed be your name." Worship is a holy privilege!

One of Christianity's most profound authors, A. W. Tozer, wrote, "God has been abridged, reduced, modified, edited, changed and amended until He is no longer the God whom Isaiah saw, high and lifted up."[7] I think many would agree today that in our well-meaning efforts to make God more approachable, we've lost the wonder of His holiness. When Isaiah saw the Lord high and lifted up, he fell face down before Him. Dear friend, would you dare to ask God to give you deeper awareness and awe for His holiness? In fact, why don't you pause for a moment? Get on your knees. Bow your head. Confess to the Lord that you've lost a bit of the wonder of His holiness. Ask God to give you a picture of the throne room. Ask the Holy Spirit to create in you an awakening to God's holiness, glory, and majesty. Trust me. It's a prayer He loves to answer.

Why is this invitation so important?

Jesus knows that we become like what we worship. If our view of God is distorted, we will worship the wrong image. Therefore, it is foundational that we pray for clear revelation of God's character. His character is revealed in His names. When we worship, looking at the names of God, we can be sure we are worshiping God in spirit and in truth. In so doing we will be changed. We simply can't worship God and not be transformed in the process. His invitation to us is an invitation to intimacy with Him.

REFLECT

Imagine the picture that Isaiah saw and heard in the throne room. Describe it in your own words here.

When you think of God's holiness, does it feel inviting or terrifying?

How might a deeper understanding of God's holiness draw you into deeper intimacy with Him?

APPLY

When you think of Isaiah's vision, how does that scene in heaven impact you personally? What is God inviting you to do?

PRAY

Holy One, I bow before You and echo the praise that resounds in heaven around the throne continually, "Holy, holy, holy is the LORD Almighty!" As I bow here before You, my mind can't comprehend all that You are, and yet, I long for a more intimate relationship with You. Oh, Holy Spirit, bring my heart into perfect alignment with the heart of Jesus. Fill me with renewed passion for Your holiness in my life. (Based on Rev. 4:8–11.)

Now It's Your Turn

Write out a prayer in the space below, asking God to heal any wounds from your childhood religious upbringing. Ask Him to give you deeper understanding of His holiness but also His love. The truth is, His holiness and love go hand in hand.

LISTEN

"Behold Him Now," sung by Anna Byrd (Gateway Worship)[8]

MEMORIZE

Write out, "Ascribe to the LORD the glory due his name; worship the LORD in the splendor of his holiness" (Ps. 29:2).

GOD IDENTIFIES HIMSELF AS "I AM"

As I write this, it is almost the beginning of the Advent season. Christmas is my very favorite holiday, and I never want my heart to grow cold to the wonder of the incarnation. I often start listening to Christmas carols by the end of October. One of my favorites is "O Come, All Ye Faithful." My favorite line in that great Christmas hymn is, "Word of the Father, now in flesh appearing."[9] Ah, Jesus came to reveal the Father to us in one perfect word. When He teaches us to pray "Hallowed be Your name," He is inviting us to come and adore God for being the glorious and indescribable I Am.

Remember Moses? Moses was out in the desert taking care of sheep after fleeing Egypt because he had committed a crime. As he was caring for the sheep, he had a profound holy experience with God.

He saw a burning bush that was on fire but not consumed by the fire. Moses went over for a closer look, and that's when God spoke from the bush. God invited

Moses to take off his shoes, instructing him that he was standing on holy ground. From there, God called Moses to lead His people out of Egypt.

Today, we're going to take a closer look at that story and consider what the implications are for our worship walk.

EXPLORE

READ EXODUS 3

Imagine how intrigued Moses felt by a bush on fire that was not burning up. How does God respond when Moses goes to the bush?

How did God identify Himself to Moses? Write out verse 6 in the space below.

What was Moses' response? How is his response to God similar to the response we saw in Isaiah yesterday?

God then commissioned Moses to lead His captive people out of Egypt (Ex. 3:10).

Part of God's plan for Israel in calling them out from Egypt was for them to be able to worship Him freely. It's ironic because, even today, He calls us to worship Him freely, but our worshiping Him in spirit and truth also sets us free. When we worship God in truth, we worship Him for the truth about who He is according to Scripture. When we worship Him in spirit, we yield our spirits to His Spirit. As we worship Him authentically, He provides an exodus from our own captivity.

Moses was filled with self-doubt. He questioned God, wondering out loud, "Who am I that I should go to Pharoah and bring the Israelites out of Egypt?" (Ex. 3:11). Then Moses argued, *But what if the Israelites ask me who sent me? What if they asked me Your name?*

Then God spoke to Moses, "I Am who I Am" (Ex. 3:14–15). In your Bible, circle the words "I Am who I Am."

God also identified Himself as the Lord. This is the English translation of the Hebrew *Yahweh*. Both of these names speak to the absolute self-existence and personal nature of God. In other words, He is the uncreated, self-existent, all sustaining, personal Holy God. The name "Yahweh" was considered so holy by the Jewish people that it was spoken by the high priest publicly only once a year on the Day of Atonement (Num. 6:22–27).

Jesus came to earth as the "living Word" to show us the Father. In the words of author and Bible teacher Warren Wiersbe, Jesus "literally 'fleshed out'" I Am.[10] Throughout the gospel of John, we see Jesus revealing the Father through His I Am statements: I am the bread of life, I am the door, I am the vine, I am the good shepherd, and I am the resurrection and the life. Each of these I Am statements meets us at our point of need and draws us into worshiping Christ as the God incarnate. In another Bible study I wrote, titled *Who Do You Say That I Am?*,[11] I focus on the following "I Am" statements of Christ:

- I Am He—John 4:26
- I Am the Bread of Life—John 6:35
- I am the Good Shepherd—John 10:11
- I Am the Light—John 8:12
- I Am the Resurrection and the Life—John 11:25
- I Am the Way, the Truth, and the Life—John 14:6
- I Am the Vine—John 15:5
- I Am the Living One—Revelation 1:17

REFLECT

READ EXODUS 3:15 ONCE AGAIN.

How does this verse underscore how worshiping God transforms generations? How might your worship transform generations coming up behind you?

As we reflect on the story of Moses and the burning bush, there are several principles we can draw for how to worship the Lord in our own personal lives.

ADORE HIM.

What posture did Moses use to adore God when God spoke to Him? What does it look like for you to spend time adoring God each day?

MAGNIFY HIM BEFORE UNBELIEVERS.

How did Moses magnify the great I Am before Pharaoh? How might you magnify God's glory before your unbelieving friends?

OBEY AND SURRENDER TO HIM.

Moses felt terrified, but he eventually did what God asked him to do. *Do you ever feel inadequate? What does it look like for you to obey God even when you don't feel up to the task?*

APPLY

What is God's invitation to you personally today as far as making worship a part of your everyday life?

Holy One, I worship You as the great I Am, the first and the last. I fall on my face as the apostle John did. You are the One who was and is and is to come. I bow before You and exalt You as the only One who is eternally holy. Teach me how to worship and adore You daily. Take me deeper, I pray, into exalting You. I know that is where I am changed. (Based on Rev. 1:17–18.)

Now It's Your Turn

Write a prayer to the great I Am. Ask the Holy Spirit to awaken a fresh passion for worship in your life.

LISTEN

"Holy, Holy, Holy (We Bow Before Thee)," sung by Shane and Shane[12]

MEMORIZE

Review Psalm 29:2: "Ascribe to the LORD the glory due his name; worship the LORD in the splendor of his holiness."

WEEK 2 | DAY 3

THE NAME ABOVE
EVERY OTHER NAME

When my husband, Steve, and I were living overseas in the country of Sudan, I became pregnant, and we were having difficulty settling on a name. I didn't have an ultrasound, so we weren't sure if our new little nugget was a boy or a girl. After much deliberation, we settled on a girl's name, but Steve was convinced we were having a boy.

My labor pains started and because we were living overseas and because I had vivid memories of my delivery of our daughter two years prior, I was extremely hesitant to go to the hospital. However, when I was doubled over in pain, I knew I had no choice. When we got to the hospital in Khartoum, Sudan, the midwives were not thrilled with how long I had taken to arrive and began scolding me. Call me crazy, but when a woman is in labor, it's not the best time for scolding or arguing. Right?!

The next battle was that we had received permission from the doctors to have my husband present when I delivered. This was highly unusual in Sudan, and the midwives were giving me a hard time. They commanded me to start pushing, but as I said, not the best time to argue with a woman in labor! I told them in no uncertain terms that I would not push until my husband was present. Steve heard all this commotion and came marching into the room. He announced that he felt God had told him we were having a son and that his name would be "Josiah" after one of Israel's most righteous kings. With that announcement, I pushed and we delivered our beautiful son.

Our little "king," with his big blue eyes and light hair, certainly drew attention in the nursery of that Sudanese hospital.

Names are important. Throughout Jewish history, parents named their kids after relatives or according to the traits they hoped their children would develop. At times they even named them according to the traits they exhibited at birth. Remember the story of Rebekah who gave birth to twin boys? Jacob was born with his hand on his brother Esau's heel, and so his parents named him Jacob, "the trickster."

Every name of God has meaning, and each one points to one of His attributes. Today, we're going to explore worshiping Jesus Christ. We're going to look through the lens of some of His names and seek to understand why God gave Him the name that is above every other name.

EXPLORE

READ LUKE 1:26-38

Describe the story in your own words.

READ LUKE 1:31 AND MATTHEW 1:21

The angel told Mary that she was to call the baby conceived by the Holy Spirit "Jesus." The name Jesus means "the LORD IS SALVATION."[13]

What do you think is the significance of this name?

READ GALATIANS 5:1

Remember the story of God using Moses to lead the Israelites out of slavery? Jesus ushered in the new exodus, providing the way for people to be set free from the slavery of sin. How did Jesus provide for our freedom from sin?

READ LUKE 1:32-33

Beyond being our Savior, Jesus is also King. Write down how the angel described the role of Jesus to Mary as found in these verses.

READ PSALM 24:7-10

David was writing prophetically about Jesus in these verses. *How does David's poetic description compare with what the angel told Mary?*

READ PHILIPPIANS 2:9-11

The apostle Paul wrote that Jesus was given by God the name that is above every name. *Why was Jesus given this name? What does this passage teach us about the lordship and absolute authority of Jesus?*

REFLECT

As you reflect on Jesus setting you free from sin, what does that mean to you personally? How have you experienced His freedom?

As you reflect on Jesus being King, what response does this call for on your part? How does His rule show up in your life on a daily basis?

APPLY

What is God's invitation to you today?

PRAY

Lord Jesus, I bow before You, King of kings and Lord of lords. I exalt You for having the name that is above every other name, and I echo the words of Paul who wrote that at the name of Jesus every knee would bow and every tongue confess that Jesus is Lord. Thank You that You paid the price for my freedom and now I can stand confident in that freedom. I worship You as King of my life. I pray that Your glory would shine through me today. (Based on Rev. 19:16; Phil. 2:10–11.)

Now It's Your Turn

Write a prayer of worship based in Scripture praising God that you have been set free.

LISTEN

"Endless Praise," sung by Charity Gayle.[14] As you listen, imagine the chorus in heaven.

MEMORIZE

Review Psalm 29:2. See if you can say it from memory.

ADORE HIM WITH AFFECTIONATE WORDS

My husband often teases me about the first time he told me he loved me. We took a romantic walk in the snow on Christmas night. Under falling snow and twinkling lights, Steve told me he loved me. The thing is, I was so startled by his declaration that I replied, "Thank you!" That wasn't quite the response Steve was going for, but he wisely didn't push me. I didn't get the courage to tell him I loved him till about five days later. I know, right?! The poor guy! Don't worry. Now I tell him I love him all the time!

Like Steve, God longs for us to express our love for Him. He pursues us passionately and yearns for us to respond enthusiastically. Yet for many of us, expressing our love for God can feel awkward. God is so holy and so other that He can feel distant to us, and it can feel almost disrespectful to say, "I love You, Lord." Yet those are the very words our God longs to hear. He longs for our adoration and expressions of love.

Today, we're going to look at expressing our love as an act of worship. When we respond to God's invitation to worship Him, we need to respond to His overtures of love.

EXPLORE

READ JOHN 12:1-11

Where does this story take place?

Use the bullet points to describe what happened in the story.

-

-

-

-

-

Pure nard was a very valuable ointment that came from the dried roots of the plant called nard. It was often imported in alabaster boxes and was very expensive. When Mary took a pint of pure nard and poured it on Jesus' feet and let down her hair to wipe them, it was a picture of extravagant love.

READ JOHN 12:4

How did Judas react to Mary's love offering?

This would have taken place after Mary's brother Lazarus was raised from the dead. *How do you think that event influenced Mary's extravagant worship?*

READ JOHN 12:7

How does Jesus defend Mary? In what other story found in the Gospels did Jesus defend Mary? What do we learn about Mary's devotion to Jesus from these stories?

What do these verses reveal about Jesus' heart and what He desires in our worship?

REFLECT

Do you have a hard time expressing love to God in your worship? Why or why not?

How does your home church view expressing emotion in worship? What would happen if you knelt down during a Sunday morning worship service?

Do you worship in the privacy of your own home? What does that look like for you?

APPLY

Take some time to think back on your life. Make a list of sins God has forgiven you for, tragedies He's rescued you from, healing He's accomplished in your life, and the blessings He's given you. Then spend some time, on your knees if you are physically able, worshiping and praising Him for all He's done. Tell Him how much you love Him.

What is God's invitation to you today?

Lord Jesus, I love You! You are my strength, my rock, my fortress, and my deliverer. Thank You for all You've done in my life. Thank You for forgiving my sins, for rescuing me from the pit of selfishness, for blessing me with the power of Your Holy Spirit. I exalt and worship You for all You've accomplished in my life. I praise You that I can step into the future confidently because You are my Savior. Your plans are to prosper me and not harm me. Teach me to express how much I love You through my praise, my obedience, and my words of love for You. (Based on Pss. 18:1–3; 103:3; Jer. 29:11.)

Now It's Your Turn

Write out a prayer to the Lord expressing your love for Him.

LISTEN

"A Thousand Hallelujahs," sung by Brooke Ligertwood[15]

MEMORIZE

Recite Psalm 29:2.

ADORE AND ENJOY

Over the past week of considering God's invitation for us to worship Him, we have reflected on God's nature and the fact that He invites us to worship Him because, as we do, we are changed. However, today I want to draw your attention to another element of God's nature and that is that He longs for us to enjoy Him! God is a social God. He desires community with us.

Yesterday, we talked about His yearning to hear our affection. He longs for us to express our affection and tell Him that we love Him. But at times in our human thinking we can view God as rather emotionally distant. We might tell Him we love Him because we know we're supposed to, but do we really enjoy Him? Ah, that's a question that is worth pondering. Ask yourself, "Do I truly enjoy God?"

The truth is that God wants a love relationship with us.

READ PSALM 5:7

What does this verse teach us about why God invites us into His presence to bow down before Him?

God's invitation for us to worship Him is an invitation of love to us.

READ GENESIS 3:8

In this verse, we find that the man and woman heard God walking in the garden in the cool of the day. This happened after they had eaten from the tree of the knowledge of good and evil that God commanded them not to eat from. Based on their shame, they hid from God. However, before sin, they enjoyed their evening walks with God.

Pause for a moment. Imagine. They walked and talked with God, enjoying His presence and His fellowship. Don't you wonder what they talked about? Before sin, they wouldn't have been asking God to heal anyone or fix any broken relationship. They wouldn't have asked for financial needs to be met or for wrong attitudes to be corrected. They simply would have enjoyed His presence and intimate conversation with Him.

We live in a world of sin resulting in sickness, broken relationships, violence, and evil. But imagine with me putting all that aside because in Christ we have been made right with the Father. Imagine with me conversations with God where we are not asking for anything but simply enjoying His presence. What would we talk about? Perhaps the beauty of the sun glistening in a blue sky or freshly fallen snow.

Maybe we would admire the creativity with which God created the universe. Maybe we would be filled with wonder and ask Him, "Lord, what was it like to fling the stars in place?" Or, "How did it feel when the first waves of the ocean crashed on the shores?"

My point is this. Sin changed everything; yet God has made provision for us to live and enjoy Him in restored relationship here and now. What does it look like to simply enjoy God's presence? This is to be a part of our worship.

If I were to define what it means to enjoy God I would define it this way:

Enjoying God is

delighting in Him

more than in the gifts He gives.

READ PSALM 37:4

Write out the words to Psalm 37:4 in the space below. Circle the word delight. The Hebrew word for delight is anag, *which instructs us to find enjoyment in God.*[16]

When I think of finding enjoyment in someone, I think of my husband, kids, or grandkids. I create the space to be with them because they are important to me. I delight to hear their thoughts. I love spending time with them. I find great joy in simply being with them.

Unlike husbands, children, or close friends, only the Lord Himself is perfect in His love for us. He wants us to just enjoy being with Him.

What does this look like for you?

Maybe for you it means sitting quietly and simply imagining that God is holding you close and loving you. Or maybe it means taking a walk and imagining God is right beside you. As you walk, you talk with Him about the beauty of His creation. You converse about how beautiful the creation is and how it reflects God's glory.

Many of us are uptight about prayer. We wonder, "How can I power through long times of prayer without falling asleep or growing distracted?" Is it possible we've made it far too complicated? Perhaps God simply wants us to enjoy and delight in His presence. He desires for us to listen for the rhythm of His heart and to breathe in sync with Him, just enjoying His closeness.

How does tension in your life keep you from enjoying prayer?

READ PSALM 63:3

When we learn to nestle down, enjoying God's presence, our hearts will echo the words of the psalmist, David, "Your love is better than life." David spent countless hours with the Lord and as a result lived a life of adoration.

How might enjoying God's presence lead you to adoration?

REFLECT

What most often prevents you from enjoying and delighting in God's presence?

If you find you're not enjoying God's presence, what could you do about it? List a few tangible ideas in the space below:

APPLY

Create some space where you can be alone with God. Simply try sitting quietly in His presence for two minutes.

What is God's specific invitation to you personally today?

Lord Jesus, so often I go an entire day without acknowledging Your presence in my life. Forgive me, Lord! Thank You that You desire my company and that You long to be gracious to me. Father, I confess I often feel confused about what it means to enjoy You. Your Word teaches me that I am to delight myself in the Lord. Holy Spirit, open my heart to experience more deeply the presence of Christ. Increase my hunger and my thirst to spend time with You simply enjoying Your presence. (Based on Isa. 30:18; Ps. 37:4; Matt. 5:6.)

Now It's Your Turn

Write out a prayer asking the Lord to increase your delight in Him.

LISTEN

"Jesus the Beloved," sung by Lindy Cofer and Laura Hackett[17]

MEMORIZE

Recite Psalm 29:2.

THE
INVITATION
TO SURRENDER

"Your Kingdom Come,
Your Will Be Done"

MATTHEW 6:10

UNDERSTANDING LORDSHIP

A few years ago, when Steve and I were traveling in London, we made a stop at Buckingham Palace. Now to be clear, we didn't go in and have tea with the Queen! Like all the other tourists, we hung around outside the palace gates and watched the guards pace back and forth.

As Americans, we don't understand monarchies very well, but we still seem to be obsessed with royalty. Right? This is why the two TV series *The Crown* and *Downton Abbey* have been so popular. And there are countless magazines with articles about the British royals. We wonder, "What is it really like in the palace? What would it be like to be royalty? What do they do in there all day, and do kings and queens really have any authority, or are they only figureheads?"

Culturally, we can't really relate. We value freedom and independence. We bring our American, independent, casual mindset to the whole thought of a monarchy. That's fine, I suppose, as far as how we view earthly monarchies; but in the kingdom of

Christ, we must not view the lordship of Christ through our cultural lens. Now her Majesty Queen Elizabeth II bows before His Majesty, the King of kings and the Lord of lords, Jesus Christ.

When we are born again and become citizens of Christ's kingdom, we submit to His rule and reign in our lives. When we pray for His kingdom to come and for His will to be done, we are praying for His authority to rule over our lives.

This week we'll be looking at the invitation for us to surrender.

EXPLORE

READ MATTHEW 6:9-10

Write those words in the space below. Then circle the words "your," "kingdom," and "will."

Often we have mistaken beliefs about the kingdom of God. We're not alone. The Jews living at the time of Jesus also had misconceptions about the kingdom of God and the role of the Messiah. The Jewish people knew from prophecy that a Messiah would come, but they imagined him as a mighty warrior who would free them from their enemy and reestablish Israel's kingdom under the Davidic dynasty.[1] When King Herod ruled over Judea under the Roman Empire, he understood that the Messiah the Jews expected was to be another king and therefore a rival to himself. He saw the baby born in a manger as a threat to his rule.

After the famous miracle where Jesus fed the five thousand, the crowds who followed Him wanted to make Him king (John 6:15).

The kingdom of God can feel confusing. What exactly is it? The kingdom is where Christ rules and reigns. In the future, Christ will return to earth and set up a literal kingdom where He will establish justice and peace (see Matt. 20:20–28; Rev. 20:4–6). However, there is also a present kingdom where Christ rules through "those who receive God's abundant provision of grace and the gift of righteousness" (Rom. 5:17). The kingdom is both then and now. This is important for us to understand if we are to receive Christ's invitation to surrender and pray with authenticity, "Your kingdom come, Your will be done." Yet for many of us, we have felt confused over the nature of Christ's kingdom.

Even after the resurrection, there were misconceptions about the kingdom the Messiah would establish. The problem is, if we misinterpret the kingdom, we may miss the presence of Christ in our lives now. This is what happened on the road to Emmaus.

READ LUKE 24:13-35

In this intriguing story, two of Jesus' followers, Cleopas and one other, were walking to a village called Emmaus. As they walked, Jesus Himself came up and walked with them, but they didn't recognize Him.

Why do you think the two followers of Jesus didn't recognize Him as He walked with them?

READ LUKE 24:21

Circle the words "but we had hoped" in your Bible.

What were these two followers of Jesus expecting from Jesus as the Messiah?

How do we respond today as followers of Jesus when our Messiah doesn't meet our expectations?

REFLECT

In what ways has Christ shown up as your Messiah that are different than you expected?

How might your dashed expectations make you hesitant to pray, "Your kingdom come, Your will be done"?

God's kingdom is much bigger than our little kingdoms, communities, or countries. *How might asking God for a deeper understanding of His kingdom stretch you?*

APPLY

How is God inviting you to change today?

PRAY

Lord Jesus, I confess I haven't really understood Your kingdom. Often, I have felt confused about Your lordship over my life. I tend to race into Your throne room with my long list of requests, forgetting that You want me to pray that Your lordship will rule over my life. Oh, Holy Spirit, change my heart. Make me willing to bow and surrender even when I don't understand Your ways. Help me not to miss the beauty of Your presence when You don't show up as I expect. I lay every expectation down before You and ask You to fill me with a renewed heart of surrender.

Now It's Your Turn

Write out a prayer of confession to the Lord and ask for a renewed spirit of surrender.

LISTEN

"Simple Kingdom," sung by Bryan & Katie Torwalt and Cody Carnes[2]

MEMORIZE

Galatians 2:20: "I have been crucified with Christ and I no longer live, but Christ lives in me. The life I now live in the body, I live by faith in the Son of God, who loved me and gave himself for me."

WEEK 3 | DAY 2

THE PRIORITIES
OF THE KINGDOM

Yesterday, we began our week by looking at the concept of the kingdom. We talked about how, throughout church history, there has been lots of confusion over the kingdom and what it means for us as believers to be a part of Christ's kingdom.

Today, we're going to look at the priorities of Christ's kingdom and why it is so important that we surrender to His priorities rather than our own. Timothy Keller aptly said, "The Kingdom is a way of life."[3] The question then is, "What are Christ's priorities for our lives in His kingdom?" That's the question we're going to answer today.

Before we get started, it's important that you remember that the kingdom of God is only here partially now. It will be realized fully when Christ rules in perfect justice on the new earth.

READ MATTHEW 5:17-48

These verses are a part of Jesus' Sermon on the Mount. If ever there was a description of the priorities of the kingdom, this sermon is it! Through the Sermon on the Mount, Jesus says over and over again, "You have heard it said, but I say unto you." Fill out the chart below. In each space, record each "You have heard it said" statement. Then record a statement summarizing the priority of the kingdom.

Here's an example to get you started:

YOU HAVE HEARD IT SAID	PRIORITY OF THE KINGDOM
"You shall not commit adultery" (v. 27)	Purity in our thought life (vv. 28–30)

READ LUKE 6:20-26, 46-48

These verses are the apostle Luke's description of Jesus' words on the Sermon on the Mount. Compare our culture's priorities with the priorities of Christ's kingdom as found in these verses.

OUR CULTURE'S PRIORITIES	CHRIST'S KINGDOM PRIORITIES
Power	
Wealth	
Success	
Status	

Friend, the truth is, our own kingdoms and priorities must be demolished in Christ's kingdom. Even our American values of freedom and independence must bow to the King of kings. The great theologian G. Campbell Morgan wrote:

> Therefore a man must be prepared to do violence to all his own wit and wisdom and cleverness, and be assured that the method of preaching the Gospel to the poor, and healing the sick, and opening blind eyes, and refusing to gather an army, and failing to call together a parliament, are the real methods of the Kingdom.[4]

When we pray "Your kingdom come, Your will be done," we are in essence praying, "Lord, bring my will into perfect alignment with Your will. Help me to prioritize what matters to You. May kingdom values—forgiveness, being humble and poor in spirit, letting go of my need for affirmation and accolades—mark my life. May I live a life of quiet submission bowing to Your desires over my own."

REFLECT

As you reflect on the values of the kingdom as opposed to the values of our current culture, in your opinion, which kingdom value most conflicts with the values of this world?

In Matthew 4:17, Jesus said, "Repent, for the kingdom of heaven has come near." Repentance is an invitation to reconsider or change your perspective. *In light of Christ's kingdom values, where might He be inviting you to repent?*

Draw several circles in the space below depicting different kingdoms in your life. Circles might include the kingdom of family, the kingdom of your inner life, the kingdom of your professional life, and the kingdom of your community life. In each circle, write one area where you need to surrender to God's kingdom ideals.

APPLY

What is God inviting you to do as a result of understanding His kingdom more fully?

PRAY

King Jesus, I praise You that Your kingdom resides in those like me. Thank You for the sense of purpose Your kingdom brings to my life. I praise You that Your kingdom is bigger than my little life or aspirations. Help me remember that at times I won't understand Your ways, but I must bow my will to Yours. I bow before You now and echo Jesus' prayer, "Not my will but yours be done." (Based on Matt. 5:3; 26:39.)

Now It's Your Turn

Write out a prayer of worship, praising God that Jesus is King.

LISTEN

"Lord of It All," sung by Maggie Reed (The Belonging Co)[5]

MEMORIZE

Write out Galatians 2:20 on an index card, and then post it somewhere where you'll see it often.

WHO IS THIS KING?

Singer and songwriter Rich Mullins had a profound impact during the 1990s. I loved his music, and God used it powerfully in my life. The story is told that at his concerts people would visit his merch table and often ask, "How can I find God's will for my life?" Rich listened attentively, and then he would offer an "unexpected perspective." He would reply, "I don't think finding God's plan for you has to be complicated. . . . God's will is that you love him with all your heart and soul and mind, and also that you love your neighbor as yourself. Get busy with that, and then, if God wants you to do something unusual, he'll take care of it. Say, for example, he wants you to go to Egypt. . . . If that's the case, he'll provide eleven jealous brothers and they'll sell you into slavery."[6]

When I read that story, it made me smile. I have often heard people obsess over finding God's will when the bigger question really is: "Are we willing to do God's will?" Others have confided in me that they are afraid to ask God what His will is for fear He will send them to some dark corner of the earth and their lives will be lived out in misery. It can, in the words of N. T. Wright, feel like a "risky, crazy prayer of submission and commission."[7] However, to pray this risky prayer, we must remember who God is as King of our lives.

EXPLORE

READ PSALM 24:8, 10

The psalmist asks, "Who is this King of glory?" Jesus came as the answer to this question. N. T. Wright says, "If you want to know who God is, look at Jesus."[8] I love that quote because it reminds us that God is knowable. We know Him and enjoy intimate relationship with Him through Jesus.

READ COLOSSIANS 1:15-18

If we are going to dare to surrender to the King of glory, we have to understand His nature. *When you think of Jesus, what specific attributes come to mind? List them in the space below:*

READ PHILIPPIANS 2:5-8

What is one word from this passage that describes Jesus' character?

Jesus is a humble King. He had absolute trust in our Father's love. David wrote about the love of our Father in Psalm 103.

How does the psalmist David describe God's love in this psalm? List below some specific character traits of God's love.

God's will for you is an expression of His love for you. Rev. Robert Law, writing in the early 1900s, wrote, "God is Love. The will of God is pure, unchangeable, holy Love working together for the highest goal of every creature"[9] How profound. However, even though we can work to understand God's nature, we still may not always understand His decisions. Yet, in response to His love for us, we must surrender and trust that He loves us completely.

REFLECT

Reflect on God's love for you personally. When was the last time you felt deeply and categorically loved by God? Describe the feelings you experienced.

When you think of the word "surrender," what images come to your mind?

If you were fully able to relax in God's love, how might that change your desire to surrender?

APPLY

Ask our Father to give you a deeper experience of His love today. Ask that you might know His love more completely and that you might be able to relax in His love.

PRAY

Lord Jesus, I pray that my roots would sink down deeper into Your love and absolute goodness. I pray that Your Holy Spirit would awaken my heart to understand more fully how wide and long and high and deep is the love of Christ for me. I pray that my heart would be so deeply planted in this truth that I am able to relax and delight in doing Your will. May Your love flow out of me to others so that I might love my neighbor as myself and in such do Your will with joy. (Based on Jer. 17:8; Eph. 3:17–19; Matt. 22:37–39.)

Now It's Your Turn

Write a prayer asking God to plant you deeply in His love so that even when the storms of life come, you will remain strong.

LISTEN

"King Jesus," sung by Brooke Ligertwood[10]

MEMORIZE

Write out Galatians 2:20 from memory.

NOT MY WILL, BUT YOURS BE DONE

Oswald Chambers wrote that "no one is ever united with Jesus Christ until he is willing to relinquish not sin only, but his whole way of looking at things."[11] So true! God's greatest desire is that the Holy Spirit would bring our hearts into total alignment with Christ's. We are to become like Christ and united with Christ.

Prayer isn't just about getting what we want from God, but rather learning to enjoy God and becoming united with Him. The only way this is possible is for us to surrender and release our will in favor of His. Only then do we enjoy hope and the richness of our relationship with Christ. When we pray "Your kingdom come, Your will be done," we are in essence joining Jesus in the garden of Gethsemane and crying with Him, "Not my will, but yours be done." This is the prayer of relinquishment.

Author Richard Foster wrote about the prayer of relinquishment in his profound book *Prayer: Finding the Heart's True Home*. Foster wrote that "we begin to enter into a grace-filled releasing of our will and a flowing into the will of the Father.

It is the prayer of relinquishment that moves us from the struggling to the releasing."[12] Friend, until we truly understand the prayer of relinquishment, we cannot be fully united with Christ. Let's take a deeper look.

EXPLORE

READ MARK 14:32-42

Imagine Jesus kneeling in the garden of Gethsemane. He is distraught and in utter agony as He considers the cross. Describe Jesus' emotional state in a few sentences below.

What was Jesus' longing in His prayer?

What was His relinquishment?

We must be careful to not view the prayer of relinquishment as trite thinking, "Oh sure, I'll pray not my will, but yours be done!" The prayer of relinquishment comes only with a struggle. The genuine prayer comes from a heart desperate for her own way, yet willing to lay down desires in favor of God's ways. Yet even though there is a struggle, we relinquish with hope. You see, friend, every time we echo Jesus' prayer, "Not my will, but yours be done," we are transformed a tiny bit more into the image of Christ.

Foster describes this transformation so vividly:

> Little by little we are changed by this daily crucifixion of the will. Changed, not like a tornado changes things, but like a grain of sand in an oyster changes things. New graces emerge: new ability to cast our care upon God, new joy at the success of others, new hope in a God who is good.[13]

READ LUKE 22:44

Scripture teaches that Jesus Himself struggled with God the Father's will. His sweat fell like drops of blood as He surrendered. Doctors tell us that there is a condition called hematohidrosis, which is a rare condition where the body literally sweats drops of blood.[14] In any case, we see that Jesus was in extreme emotional anguish. Yet as He knelt before the Father, He cried, "Not my will, but yours be done." This is the most profound and beautiful of all prayers of relinquishment. Jesus surrendered to the Father's will and went to the cross so that we could be made right with God.

"For our sins, He suffers beneath the burden of that unanswered prayer,"[15] author Andrew Murray wrote. At times we are tempted to think no one has experienced the unanswered prayers that we have. But that is a lie. Jesus Himself experienced unanswered prayer in the most desperate prayer of His life. Yet there He modeled for us the raw, heartfelt, prayer of relinquishment.

With the prayer of relinquishment comes the promise of provision.

Provision might mean the grace to endure rather than receiving what we desire. Or provision could come in an unexpected form or relief. How provision comes is up to God. However, every time you open your hands and relinquish, His promise of provision is there.

READ GENESIS 22:1-18

Circle in your Bible the words in verse 8, "God himself will provide." This is such an important principle that I want to be sure you get it! Friend, when we open our hands and relinquish our desires, God opens His hands and provides what we need.

REFLECT

Today, has been kind of a "heavy" day in that the prayer of relinquishment is not trite or easy. It comes with great struggle, yet profound reward. It's not a "victim" prayer. It's the prayer of a victor—one who completely trusts the love of God the Father.

Can you think of a time in your life when you laid down your desires and prayed, "Not my will, but yours be done"?

- Perhaps it's relinquishing your desire for a husband.
- Perhaps it's relinquishing your desire for a child.
- Perhaps it's relinquishing your desire for healing.

Write about that in the space below. Then answer, "How did God provide?"

Sometimes God doesn't provide in the exact ways we think He will. *How has God met you in your disappointment?*

APPLY

What is God's invitation to you personally today in the realm of relinquishment?

PRAY

Father God, help me to remember today how deeply You love me. Remind me that Your will is always good even when I don't understand. In the different struggles of life, help me to open my hands and to echo the cry of Jesus in the garden, "Not my will, but yours be done." I praise You, Lord, that I can trust You to be good. I thank You that You work out all things for good in my life because I love You. When disappointment clouds my joy, help me to surrender to hope, not out of fear, but out of love. I rest in Your will today. (Based on Luke 22:42; Ps. 107:1; Rom. 8:28.)

Now It's Your Turn

Write out your own prayer of surrender to God in the space below.

LISTEN

"Yes (Obedience)," sung by David and Nicole Binion and Madison Grace Binion[16]

MEMORIZE

Review Galatians 2:20.

ON EARTH AS IT IS IN HEAVEN

The evening news these days is anything but encouraging. Coronavirus updates continue to fill our feeds, people are more polarized than ever, and mental health issues have grown exponentially. Many businesses are struggling and can't find enough workers to hire. Inflation has risen and the divide between rich and poor is greater than ever. Certainly this is not the way God's kingdom runs in heaven.

God has bridged the gulf between heaven and earth through these gifts: "His inspired Word, his beloved Son, and the Holy Spirit."[17] Yet, the question remains, "How do we as God's people get on board with God's forever plan and cooperate with Him to bring heaven and earth together?"

We begin with the prayer, "Your will be done, on earth as it is in heaven." We yield ourselves to enter partnership with God to accomplish His plan of bringing redemption to humanity. We offer ourselves to love others the way He did, and we live out the gospel before a dying world.

EXPLORE

READ GENESIS 2:18-15; 8-20

How did Adam work in partnership with God?

Before sin entered the world, Adam and Eve worked in seamless partnership with God. There was no fear, anxiety, or worry. There was no competition or the desire to change God's mind. Humans lived to do the will of God. With sin came fear to do the will of God. But Jesus came to show us the grace of God.

READ MATTHEW 11:28-30

Jesus invited us to enter partnership with Him, joining Him in His mission of bringing God's love to mankind. When we enter partnership with Jesus, we discover He is not a harsh taskmaster. In these verses, we see three invitations: come, take, and learn. Describe what each invitation entails and the promise that goes with each in the space below.

COME

TAKE

LEARN

READ ROMANS 11:33-12:2

I grew up in a very strict, fundamentalist home. For years, I had a problem with Romans 12:1–2. I had memorized it as a child under threat and felt that giving my body as a sacrifice meant adults could do whatever they wanted with me. It wasn't until many years later when I memorized Romans 11:33–36 that I understood that surrendering our lives in order to be used by God was a response to His love and wisdom.

As you read through these verses, what can you discern about God's will?

REFLECT

As you consider the phrase "on earth as it is in heaven," how might God want you to partner with Him to bring His will to earth?

What most often stops you from surrendering to God's will?

How has studying God's kingdom changed you this week?

APPLY

What is one action you will put into place as a result of this week's study?

PRAY

Lord Jesus, I yield myself to You to be used however You see fit to further Your kingdom. I pray that You would take my life and let it be used to bring glory to Your name. May others be introduced to Jesus because of my life story. I relinquish all my hopes and dreams for You to sort through. I pray that I would exchange my will for Yours in all things. Bring my spirit into perfect unity with Your Spirit, I pray, so that I might think, and act and love like Jesus. (Based on Rom. 12:1–2.)

Now It's Your Turn

Write your own prayer in the space below, yielding yourself to be used by God however He pleases.

LISTEN

"Wouldn't It Be Like You," sung by Bryan & Katie Torwalt[18]

MEMORIZE

Review Galatians 2:20.

THE INVITATION TO ASK AUDACIOUSLY

"Give Us Today
Our Daily Bread"

MATTHEW 6:11

INVITED TO TRUST HIM FOR PROVISION

During a particularly rough season of ministry, Steve and I did not know how we would make it financially. We asked the Lord if we should sell our house, and though His answer didn't make sense to us, God said no. His recurring invitation was for us to trust Him for provision. Every morning in my early worship times with Jesus, the cry of my heart was, "Lord, teach me to trust You more!" Every time I felt the temptation to fear, I praised Him for His faithfulness.

One night as we were getting ready for bed, Steve checked his email. Honestly, I was not a fan of Steve checking email before bed. I think that's generally a terrible idea. However, on this particular night, as I was lying in bed reading and trying to wind down, Steve said, "Beck! You're not going to believe this! Someone just anonymously gave ten thousand dollars to our nonprofit."

What a relief! As I fell asleep that night, I heard the voice of Jesus whisper quietly in my ear, "Becky, rest. I've got this. Trust Me to provide."

God had the same challenge for the children of Israel wandering in the desert. When they were tempted to think God had abandoned them, God rained down manna from heaven daily. Now open your Bible to Exodus 16.

EXPLORE

READ EXODUS 16:1–35

In the space below, list the events of the story using bullet points.

How would you describe the attitude of the Israelites?

What was God's provision in the morning?

When the people saw the manna they asked, "What is it?" Sometimes, like the Israelites, we don't recognize God's provision.

READ EXODUS 16:13-19

What was God's provision in the evening?

Why do you think God gave the people such specific instructions for gathering the manna and not keeping it overnight?

As we think about the Lord's provision for Israel in this story, there are some truths that shed light on what Jesus taught us to pray in Matthew 6:11: "Give us today our daily bread." At the time Jesus instructed us to pray for our daily bread, bread was the most basic food of life. Every family was careful to bake bread and to have it readily available.

After Jesus fed the five thousand with a little boy's lunch, the people following Him wanted to see another miraculous show. Jesus made a profound statement.

READ JOHN 6:35

Write Jesus' statement in the space below.

When Jesus referred to Himself as the Bread of Life, He was in essence saying, "All that you need, I myself will provide."

When He invited us to pray for our daily bread, the term for "daily" is interesting. It is used nowhere else in the New Testament. It is not found in Hellenistic literature nor in the Septuagint. Many Bible scholars feel Jesus coined a new word. The best translation seems to be "coming day." R. T. Kendall writes, "If prayed in the morning, it means today. If prayed in the evening, it means tomorrow."[1]

When we pray "Give us today our daily bread," we are asking the Lord to provide for our physical, emotional, and spiritual needs. Psychologist Abraham Maslow (1908–1970) proposed the hierarchy of needs. At the bottom of his pyramid were basic things like food, shelter, and sleep. The next level up were needs like safety and security. Then belonging needs: feeling loved and accepted. Finally, at the top, Maslow listed self-actualization.[2] As believers, instead of talking about self-actualization, we might believe the top of the pyramid is stepping fully into our anointing and calling to live our life on purpose for God.

I remember learning about Maslow's hierarchy in college and, later in life, coming to the conclusion that Jesus Himself promises to provide for all those needs. What an amazing Savior we have! He invites us to ask audaciously, that all our needs be met daily!

REFLECT

Listed below are three principles from the story of God providing manna. Below each principle, write a few sentences for how this speaks to your personal situation.

HIS PROVISION WAS DAILY.

HIS PROVISION WAS ABUNDANTLY ENOUGH FOR EACH DAY.

HIS PROVISION WAS TO BUILD TRUST IN HIS CARE.

As you reflect on your own life, why is it hard for you to trust God for provision?

READ PSALM 78:18-35

In what ways are you tempted like the Israelites to doubt God's goodness and put Him to the test?

How has God lovingly shown you His faithful provision through the years?

How does celebrating His provision increase your ability to trust Him more?

All through the Scriptures, from Genesis to Revelation, God's message to us is the same, "Trust Me to provide." He provides for our physical needs in terms of food, finances, or healing. While He may not always provide in the way you wish, He does promise that He will supply all our needs (Phil. 4:19). He also made provision for our spiritual needs by providing for our redemption.

How did God provide for our redemption?

APPLY

What is God's invitation to you personally today?

Lord Jesus, I praise You, that You invite me to trust You and to commit all my plans to You. Lord, honestly, trust seems like a lifelong journey for me. At times, I trust You so well, resting in Your care. At other times, not so much. I praise You Lord that You alone are worthy of my trust. Thank You that You have always provided for me exactly what I have needed. Though at times I may not understand Your ways, I ask that You strengthen my heart with deeper faith as I continue to call on You for what I need. (Based on Prov. 3:5–6.)

Now It's Your Turn

Write out a prayer asking God to increase your ability to provide for your needs.

LISTEN

"Honey in the Rock," sung by Brooke Ligertwood and Brandon Lake[3]

MEMORIZE

Luke 11:9: "So I say to you: Ask and it will be given to you; seek and you will find; knock and the door will be opened to you."

THE INVITATION TO ASK PERSISTENTLY

One year, we went on a vacation in Florida and took our kids to Disney World. On the last night of the vacation, after a long day at Disney, we were tucking the two littlest in bed, and our Stefanie (six at the time) starting sobbing. Earlier that day each child had chosen a souvenir from the Disney store. Keri (then four) had chosen a stuffed baby Minnie Mouse. At the store, Stef had debated about whether she also wanted the baby Minnie Mouse. She had decided she was "too big" for such a toy. The only problem? When we tucked her in that night, she had deep regret, and she sobbed uncontrollably. She wanted to go back to the Disney store even though it was nine o'clock at night. We finally got her settled, and after a lot of weeping, Stef fell asleep.

Around 10 p.m., Steve grabbed our car keys and headed to the Disney store. He actually went to three Disney stores that night, but around 10:45, he triumphantly walked into the hotel with a baby Minnie Mouse. The next morning there was a grand celebration as Steve handed Stef the stuffed toy.

Parenting experts might disagree with the way Steve handled that situation. But in that moment, Steve gave Stef a vivid picture of her heavenly Father's love for her. To this day, Stef, though now a grown woman with four kids, still remembers that moment.

Here's the thing, friend; God invites us to ask for audacious requests and to ask persistently. He *doesn't* get tired of our persistence. He loves and honors it!

We are to keep coming and continue pressing in with our requests. D. L. Moody wrote, "Some people think God does not like to be troubled with our constant coming and asking. The only way to trouble God is not to come at all."[4] The bottom line is that God honors persistence and strengthens our faith as we persevere in prayer.

Let's take a look at a story that illustrates this.

EXPLORE

READ MARK 10:46-52

Detail the story events below using bullet points. For example:

• Jesus is on His way to Jerusalem passing through Jericho.

When Bartimaeus called to Jesus, he cried out, "Jesus, Son of David." This is significant because it is a direct reference to Jesus being the promised Messiah. In Matthew 22:41–45, Jesus questions the Pharisees about their understanding of the Messiah. When He asked them, "Whose son is the Messiah?" their immediate answer was, "The son of David." It was a well-known truth about the Messiah that He would indeed come from the lineage of David and was often called "the son of David." Even a blind beggar knew that the Messiah would come as "the Son of David." When Bartimaeus cries out to Jesus, recognizing Him as the son of David, this man demonstrated his belief that Jesus was the promised Messiah, and as such, He had the power to heal.

Write out the question that Jesus asked Bartimaeus in the space below. Why is this question significant?

What part do you think faith had in Bartimaeus receiving his answer?

How did Bartimaeus demonstrate persistence?

What might have happened had Bartimaeus given up?

READ MATTHEW 7:7-8

In the Greek, the word "ask" and "seek" are in the continuous present tense. What does that mean? It means Jesus is inviting us to ask and keep on asking! Seek and keep on seeking! In other words, don't stop!

I love the New Living Translation of these verses, "Keep on asking, and you will receive what you ask for. Keep on seeking, and you will find. Keep on knocking, and the door will be opened to you. For everyone who asks, receives. Everyone who seeks, finds. And to everyone who knocks, the door will be opened." Friend, Jesus invites us to persistent asking. Keep it up!

READ LUKE 18:1-8

Widows at the time of Jesus rarely received justice. The widow in Jesus' story goes to the town judge and begs him to give her justice. Finally, she is granted justice because she keeps bothering the judge. Then Jesus says, "Will not God bring about justice for his chosen ones, who cry out to him day and night?" (Luke 18:7). This story honors the persistence of the widow. However, beyond our persistence, Jesus is persistent. He is our persistent intercessor. An intercessor is one who comes as a mediator between two parties for the purpose of justice. Jesus persistently cries out to the Father for justice on our behalf day and night (see Heb. 7:25). Though we are justified through Christ's blood atonement, Jesus' continual intercession before the Father "applies what the atonement accomplishes."[5]

REFLECT

Do you consider yourself to be a persistent person or a person who easily gives up? How might this personality trait impact your prayer life?

Have you ever felt afraid that perhaps you were annoying God by coming to Him so often with the same request? How does the teaching today quiet this fear?

As you think about our memory verse for this week (Heb. 4:16), what does bold-ness have to do with persistence?

When God seems silent, how do you most often respond?

What would it take in your life to be more consistent and persistent in the realm of prayer?

APPLY

What did God speak to you today?

Lord Jesus, thank You for inviting me to come boldly into the throne room to ask You for specific needs. I've been taught along the way that persistence can be annoying. Oh Lord, I now realize that You love persistence and You honor perseverance. Fill me with renewed determination in my prayer life. Help me erase the messages I've received and realize how deeply You value persistence. Holy Spirit, when it feels like my prayers aren't being answered, strengthen my faith and my determination to keep asking until You say, "Stop." (Based on Heb. 4:16 and the story Jesus told in Luke 11:1–4.)

Now It's Your Turn

Write out a prayer of praise thanking God that He never tires of our persistence.

LISTEN

"God Really Loves Us," sung by Passion, Chidima, and Crowder[6]

MEMORIZE

Write out the words to Luke 11:9.

WEEK 4 | DAY 3

INVITED TO PRAY
WITH OTHERS
AND FOR OTHERS

As I was writing this, all eyes were on Ukraine. Russia had invaded, and we sat glued to our screens.

The world has been shocked at Russia's relentless bombing of Ukraine. The humanitarian crisis that unfolded as a result has been horrifying. The very first news reports told of people hiding underground in subways and basements crying out for the world to help them. In a local hospital where children were too ill to be evacuated, one mother told a reporter that they'd run out of bread and juice for their children. Millions have fled Ukraine or have been displaced. They are desperate for the world to see their need.

As we've watched horrific scenes unfold, my mind keeps asking, "What is the church's collective responsibility?" Certainly, at the very least, we are to intercede on their behalf. What does Jesus' invitation for us to ask audaciously mean as far as praying for others? I believe it means to pray consistently and persistently with and for others.

EXPLORE

Read and write out the words to Matthew 6:11. Circle the word "our."

As we pray, "Give us today our daily bread," we are again reminded that we are part of a global community of believers, "the wider Christian family, and human family, standing alongside the hungry, and praying, in that sense, on their behalf."[7] While many of us have perhaps never had to go without daily bread, there are those around the globe who groan for the most basic provisions. Jesus invites us to groan with them.

When Jesus invites us to pray these words, He is inviting us to pray specifically, not only for our own needs but for the needs of those around the world. And while we plead with God to feed the hungry, He might just call us to be a part of the answer to that prayer. How can we pray, "Lord, provide bread for the hungry" if we ourselves are not willing to give of our time or money to aid hunger relief programs?

READ MATTHEW 18:19-20

Jesus invites us to pray together in unity. The Greek word for "agree" that is used here is *sumphóneó*, "to call out with."[8] Our English word "symphony" comes from *sumphóneó*. The idea is that Jesus is inviting us to gather together and lay our requests before Him in perfect harmony.

In light of this, what might be the implications of isolation and disunity within the church?

It's intriguing to me that we are not to just pray that our spiritual needs be met, but also that our physical and emotional needs be met. It seems the church has gone to extremes here in one direction or another. There are those who feel it's unspiritual to pray for our physical needs and desires; and there are those who believe following Jesus means God will make them rich and prosperous. Now don't get me wrong. You are absolutely invited to ask audaciously for your needs and the needs of others to be met. However, the prerequisite is that you seek God first.

READ MATTHEW 6:33

What is the condition Jesus teaches here for answered prayer?

When we seek God's kingdom first, we ask the Holy Spirit to bring our hearts into complete alignment with God's heart. Once our hearts are in line with His, we can be assured that what we ask for in prayer He will give. Now, this doesn't mean we should only ask for spiritual things. We are invited to pray about everything, because as a loving Father, God delights in hearing our hearts. So go ahead and bring your desires and the desires of others before Him, but continually ask Him that He would align your heart with His.

REFLECT

In the aftermath of the pandemic, physical attendance in churches and at prayer meetings has diminished.

As you reflect on Jesus' words, "Where two or three gather" (Matt. 18:20), do you feel it's important to gather in groups or just with your family watching online?

Have you ever prayed out loud with others? Why or why not?

How would you describe a dynamic prayer meeting?

In your own life, what does it look like for you to seek first the kingdom of God and His righteousness?

APPLY

What do you feel God is saying to you today?

PRAY

Lord Jesus, I praise You that You invite me to pray with others and for others with bold-ness. Thank You that as I ask audaciously, You will strengthen my faith. Father, help me to continue to gather with others to pray—whether in a small group or large group. Help me understand that You favor community and not isolation. Lord, I pray that You would teach me to be bold in praying with others. Help me understand that we seek You together. I pray that You would prompt me through your Holy Spirit to pray for others often, both in my private prayer times and in public prayer times.

Now It's Your Turn

Check the latest world news, and then write out a prayer for believers in another part of the globe.

LISTEN

"In Jesus Name (God of Possible)," sung by Katy Nichole[9]

MEMORIZE

Write out the words to Luke 11:9 from memory.

WEEK 4 | DAY 4

THE INVITATION TO LAY YOUR QUESTIONS DOWN

I remember it all so well. A young boy in our church was diagnosed with cancer. We gathered the church. People prayed. They surrounded the home of the child and prayed for hours. We all believed he was going to be healed. And yet, he died a few days later. We were crushed! As I wrestled with how to best minister to our people, I remember praying, "Lord, I don't understand, but somehow I lay my questions down at Your feet trusting that You will help me get up and encourage our people. Holy Spirit, please give me words."

In their book *Divine Disruption*, Tony Evans, Chrystal Evans Hurst, Priscilla Shirer, Anthony Evans, and Jonathan Evans authentically share wrestling with their faith as they coped with many losses of family members over a two-year time. Jonathan Evans described his disappointment when God took his mom with these words:

> If we have victory in Your name, didn't You hear us when we were praying?
> Didn't You see the people walking around my parents' house? Did You hear

the prayers of . . . churches around the world both big and small?

Where are You, Lord? Didn't You hear us calling? Why didn't You do as we asked?[10]

In the life of every believer, there will come a time when God doesn't answer your prayers as you think He should, and you will be hurled headfirst into a crisis of faith. That's what we're going to study today, because in that moment when God disappoints, you will be faced with a choice: Will you chuck your faith, or will you cling to faith though you do not understand?

EXPLORE

Scattered throughout the Scriptures, we see stories of those who prayed but God answered no. Most profound of all these stories was definitely Jesus crying out to God the Father in the garden of Gethsemane.

READ MATTHEW 26:36-46

What was Jesus' request of God the Father?

How many times did He ask?

What was His emotional state during His prayer time?

What was God the Father's answer?

READ JOHN 11:1–44

While we tend to feel elated at the resurrection that occurs in this story, Mary and Martha felt disappointed with Jesus. He didn't come when they called. When Jesus finally arrived, Lazarus was already dead. Imagine the disappointment and crisis of faith that Martha and Mary experienced. Jesus could have showed up soon after He heard that Lazarus was ill. Instead, He purposefully stayed away longer.

When He finally arrived on the scene, how did Martha and Mary respond?

In both the story of Jesus crying out to God the Father in the garden and Lazarus dying, we see the tender side of Jesus. When we don't understand God's ways, when He disappoints us with His answers, we tend to get mad or doubt God's goodness. We wonder, "Does He really answer prayer? Because it doesn't seem to be working for me!" What if instead, when we don't understand God's answer, we cling by faith to the fact that God is good and that He weeps with us? How might that help?

Pete Greig, the founder of the 24/7 prayer movement, has some rich thoughts on the questions revolving around unanswered prayer. In one talk he gave, Pete reminded listeners that some prayer goes unanswered because of God's world and the order He has already established in the universe. Some unanswered prayers are because of God's *will* and the fact that His ways are higher than ours. There are things I prayed for in my youth that today I am thankful He answered with a no. There are other unanswered prayers I simply don't understand, but I have come to trust that God's ways are higher than mine.

Finally, sometimes when we don't get the answer we desire, it is because of God's *war*. We are in a battle against the evil one. When a girl is raped, a child molested or kidnapped, or a person is murdered, that is not God's will. However, while Jesus has won the victory and will someday establish His righteous rule and reign, right now, we are in a battle. Our part in the battle is to contend in prayer. But, until Jesus comes again, evil will still be a part of our world.[11]

REFLECT

Think about a time when God said no to your prayers. Write a few sentences describing that situation in the space below and how you felt. How did you process your disappointment with God?

When you don't understand God's ways and hope seems lost, what helps you bolster your faith?

What Scriptures have been helpful to you in processing your pain and helping you to keep praying even when God feels silent?

APPLY

What questions might God be inviting you to lay at His feet?

PRAY

Lord Jesus, I remember so well the pain and disappointment I felt when I experienced _____ [describe in a couple of words your pain: e.g., the divorce, the miscarriage, the failed adoption, the betrayal of a friend, the diagnosis of cancer]. My heart echoed the cry of Martha and Mary, "If only!" If only You had stepped in, if only You had protected, if only You had answered my prayers. Father, it is at times so hard for me to trust You. I want to rest in that trust. Help me, Lord Jesus, when I don't understand Your ways, when circumstances tell me that it doesn't make sense to trust that You are weeping with me, that You love me and that someday You will right every wrong. (Based on John 11:21–45.)

Now It's Your Turn

Write out a prayer of lament, expressing your sorrow over pain and suffering.
Then praise God that someday He will right every wrong.

LISTEN

"Praise You in This Storm," sung by Natalie Grant[12]

MEMORIZE

Review Luke 11:9.

THE INVITATION
TO RECEIVE REST

I don't know about you, but for me, the COVID pandemic was a reset. I had been going hard and fast for the four years prior. Here's the thing—it wasn't sustainable.

When everything shut down, and I had long hours at home with the Lord, He began to speak to me about sustainable rhythms of rest. I felt so burned out that I met via phone with an evangelical spiritual director who I knew had a great reputation. She asked questions, read Scripture to me over the phone, listened, and together we prayed. One thing was sure: God was telling me that He wanted me to learn to embrace rest as a gift.

In addition, I started listening to Pete Scazzero's podcast, *Emotionally Healthy Leadership*. Often, Pete's podcasts are on embracing our limits, receiving rest, and living an unhurried life of prayer. The word "unhurried" gives me pause. Often, with a full daily schedule, I've raced through life instead of living an unhurried life of prayer. When I study the life of Jesus, He's never in a rush. He moved through life on purpose, for a purpose, the entire time listening to His Father. He often pulled away for times of refreshment in prayer with the Father and rested whenever needed. I needed the reminder to live an unhurried life of prayer.

I am now more convinced than ever that rest is a part of our daily bread. We are to respond to God as our loving Father, asking Him to give us our daily rest. Remember, in the words of Warren Wiersbe, "Bread represents all that we need to sustain life as we serve the Lord."[13] Our bodies, souls, and spirits need rest in order to sustain our life as we serve God. We need physical rest from the frenetic pace of our lives, but we also need spiritual rest and renewal, media rest, and creative rest. In this wonderful invitation, Jesus is beckoning us to ask for the rest we need.

EXPLORE

From Genesis to Revelation, Scripture teaches us and invites us to rest. I find it so interesting that Sabbath rest was introduced even *before* sin entered the world. In the creation story, we find that God rested on the seventh day (Gen. 2:2), thus establishing a precedent for mankind.

After the fall of Adam and Eve, work became stressful and full of striving, which makes rest even more important. As believers, we often are fine praying that God will provide for our daily needs of food, clothing, and love, and close relationships. However, we often don't ask for Him to provide rest, nor do we receive it happily when He gives it because we are reluctant to admit and embrace our limits. Let me give you an example. When I was diagnosed with breast cancer and went through an initial six-hour surgery, my body was exhausted. But I found myself feeling so useless. Most days I was lying on the couch, completely unproductive. I begged God for more energy, rather than praising Him for the rest He was giving. I received hundreds of cards from friends around the world, and do you know what most of the cards had written in them? "Be still and know that I am God!" I remember throwing one card on the floor and crying out to God, "I'm sick of being still!" Rather than embracing my limits, I was fighting them.

When Adam and Eve were in the garden, God gave one limit: "You must not eat from the tree of the knowledge of good and evil" (Gen. 2:17). One limit. Yet they pushed past the limit. That is our sin nature.

Friend, God has limited our human bodies. When you despise rest and you continually neglect the rest that your body needs, it's sin. You push past the limits God has provided. God wants you to embrace and thank Him for rest.

READ PSALM 127:2

Write the words out in the space below.

READ MATTHEW 11:28-30

These verses are not just talking about spiritual rest, they are talking about physical rest as well.

What do you think it looks like to embrace Christ's unhurried rhythms of life?

What does it look like to steward well the rest Jesus promised?

How does physical rest interact with spiritual rest?

REFLECT

According to a recent Gallup poll, 40 percent of Americans get less than the recommended amount of sleep. Medical studies have related a lack of sleep to health problems and cognitive impairment. Therefore, experts typically recommend seven to nine hours of sleep for adults.[14]

On average, about how many hours of sleep do you get per night?

If you are in a season where you are up at night with babies or toddlers, you might feel as though you are never fully rested. Hear me say, Jesus has a heart for you. While it is just a season, it is exhausting.

What are some creative ways you might be able to grab a few minutes of rest throughout the day? What might you have to let go of in order to do that?

How do you incorporate daily rest into your life? Do you view it as a gift, or do you strive to do more and be more?

How might your life change if you received rest as a gift?

APPLY

What has God spoken to you about rest today?

Lord Jesus, I praise You for the gift of rest. Thank You that You invited me to live in the "unforced rhythms of grace" (Matt. 11:28 MSG). I ask today that You would give me moments of refreshing rest through my day, even if that means pausing in the chaos around me to talk with You. I echo the words of the psalmist, "My soul finds rest in you." (Based on Matt. 11:28; Ps. 62:1.)

Now It's Your Turn

Write a prayer to the Lord thanking Him for the invitation to rest.

LISTEN

"You Can Just Rest," sung by Jenn Johnson (Bethel Worship)[15]

MEMORIZE

Review Luke 11:9.

THE INVITATION TO FIND FREEDOM THROUGH FORGIVENESS

"And Forgive Us Our Debts
as We Also Have Forgiven
Our Debtors"

MATTHEW 6:12

INTERNALIZING THE FATHER'S FORGIVENESS

R. T. Kendall, who authored *Total Forgiveness*, wrote, "The greatest need of the church today is to heed this petition."[1] In the midst of a polarized world where people seem to lack the ability to see any other view but their own, receiving forgiveness and extending forgiveness are essential. Yet even in the church, believers seem to be more divided than ever, despite Jesus saying that we will be known for our love for one another (John 13:35).

Offering forgiveness is not negotiable. In fact, this is the only invitation that includes a P.S. at the end of the Lord's Prayer: "For if you forgive other people when they sin against you, your heavenly Father will also forgive you. But if you do not forgive others their sins, your Father will not forgive your sins" (Matt. 6:14–15). Ouch! We tend to theologize this statement of Jesus, deceiving ourselves by saying, "Well, Jesus didn't *really* mean that!" Friend, I don't want to put fear in your heart or lay a guilt trip on you, but we must take these words of Jesus seriously!

Because forgiveness goes so against our human grain, we must begin by internalizing the Father's forgiveness. Experience has taught me that people who are bound in shame and have a hard time internalizing God's forgiveness, have a hard time extending that forgiveness to others. When we receive Christ's forgiveness, we are given the Holy Spirit. The Holy Spirit dwells within us. With the power of the Holy Spirit, we can do the impossible. What does it look like to internalize God's forgiveness? That's where we'll begin today.

EXPLORE

READ 1 JOHN 1:9

Write the words to 1 John 1:9 in the space below.

Many who follow Jesus consider this verse when first coming to Christ. However, this is to be a continual theme in our lives as believers. The first could read, "He is faithful and just to keep forgiving our sins." Until we reach heaven, we will continue to wrestle with our sin nature. As we grow in our relationship to the Father, we must become fast confessors. Why? Because our sin hinders our deep abiding friendship with God. It's not that He abandons us when we sin, it's that sin makes us want to hide from Him. So, as believers, we must continually lay our lives before the Holy Spirit and ask Him to bring conviction any time we sin.

READ LUKE 7:36-50

In this story Simon, a Pharisee, invited Jesus to dinner. A woman entered the dinner party and fell before Jesus, weeping and kissing His feet. Scripture identifies the woman as someone who "lived a sinful life" (v. 37). Simon, in his self-righteousness, looked at her and judged Jesus for apparently not knowing the woman had a bad reputation.

How would you describe the emotional climate in the room during this story?

How would you describe the emotions of the woman kneeling at the feet of Jesus?

What words would you use to describe Simon's attitude?

Simon is so like us as believers. It's so easy for us to justify our actions and judge others for theirs. But Jesus called Simon out and told him a story.

Write the details of the story below using bullet points:

Then Jesus asked Simon a question.

Write out Jesus' question in the space below.

Do you think the sinful woman weeping at Jesus' feet internalized God's forgiveness? Why or why not?

What about Simon? Do you think he had experienced Jesus' forgiveness in his own life? Why or why not?

REFLECT

READ 2 CORINTHIANS 7:10

How would you define godly sorrow over sin?

Think back over times in your life when you felt conviction over sin. What has godly sorrow looked like for you personally?

How would you describe the difference between guilt and shame?

Often, even though Jesus offers complete forgiveness, many continue to wrestle with guilt and shame. Some continue whether consciously or subconsciously to attempt to pay God back. There are many problems with this, but one big one is this: if we cannot receive God's forgiveness as free, we cannot extend that type of forgiveness to others. The grace you have received and internalized then flows out of you to others. Don't stop the flow by not receiving His grace yourself. Receive His forgiveness, and when you are tempted to return to shame or guilt, celebrate His grace instead. Scripture teaches that there is now no condemnation for those who are in Christ Jesus (Rom. 8:1)!

What most often prevents you from internalizing God's forgiveness? Shame? Pride? Fear?

God doesn't want you to live in shame because shame puts shackles on you. What does it look like for you to tear down the infrastructure of shame that you've constructed in your mind?

APPLY

What is Jesus speaking to you personally today?

PRAY

Lord Jesus, thank You for Your amazing grace and forgiveness. At times I confess it's too wonderful for me to completely understand and as a result, I continue to return to guilt and shame. I beat myself up for my mistakes, rather than simply embracing and celebrating Your grace. Holy One, when I sin, help me not to run from godly sorrow but to kneel at Your feet and receive Your forgiveness. Thank You that the deeper I internalize Your forgiveness the more I'll be able to extend grace to others. (Based on 1 John 1:9.)

Now It's Your Turn

Write your own prayer in the space below.

LISTEN

"Jesus Paid It All," sung by Shane & Shane[2]

MEMORIZE

Write out and begin memorizing Colossians 3:13: "Bear with each other and forgive one another if any of you has a grievance against someone. Forgive as the Lord forgave you."

FORGIVE? ARE YOU KIDDING ME?

In 1981, a Turkish man named Mehmet Ali Agca shot and injured former Pope John Paul II. Agca had been associated with a handful of radical political groups. He fired four shots with a semiautomatic pistol at the pope, critically wounding him, along with several others. The pope was immediately rushed to the hospital while Agca was apprehended. The pontiff was sixty years old at the time of the shooting and underwent five hours of surgery after losing almost three-fourths of his blood.

Just days after the shooting, in the midst of his recovery, the pope pleaded with the world to "pray for my brother [Agca] . . . whom I have sincerely forgiven." Two years later, the pope visited Agca in prison and went on to develop a genuine friendship with both the man and his family. Twenty years after the shooting, Agca was pardoned by the Italian president at the request of the pope. Years later, after Pope John Paul II's death, Agca said he felt like he had lost a brother.[3] That, my friends, is the power of forgiveness.

Author Francis Frangipane wrote, "It is inevitable that, in a world of increasing harshness and cruelty, we will at some point be hurt. But if we fail to react with love and forgiveness, if we retain in our spirit the debt the offender owes, that offense will rob our hearts of their capacity to love."[4] As I think about that terrible consequence of unforgiveness, I shudder. When we're hurt or wounded, the easiest thing in the world is to think about justice and our offender getting what he or she deserves. Jesus, however, calls us to remember that as He has forgiven us, we are to forgive others.

So, my friend, take a deep breath and ask the Holy Spirit for a heart that is open to His Word as we look at forgiving others through the rest of this week.

EXPLORE

READ MATTHEW 6:12-15

Write your first impressions of these verses in the space below.

The question that probably comes to your mind is, "Wait! Does this mean I am not saved merely by God's grace? Is my forgiveness conditional on my forgiving others?" Pause. Don't panic. But let me be clear. The apostle Paul taught that salvation is by grace alone (Eph. 2:8–9). However, we must also be very clear in this—forgiving others is imperative to our ongoing fellowship with God. When we forgive others, it is clear evidence that we have experienced the forgiveness of God. If we cannot forgive others, it would seem we have reason to question whether or not we have truly received God's forgiveness.

R. T. Kendall calls this invitation "a covenant agreement" with God. "The agreement is this: You agree to forgive them as you pray for your own forgiveness. Implied in this covenant is that you agree to be forgiven in proportion to the way you forgive."[5] We can't forgive out of our own human resources. It's impossible. However, we can forgive out of the deep well of forgiveness we've experienced.

When we choose to not forgive we are held in bondage to the perpetrator. We become the captive of that person and ultimately our bitterness can lead us to become exactly like them. It is true that hurt people hurt people.

In an interview, Pastor Louie Giglio spoke on forgiveness and the fact that so many people wrestle with forgiving their fathers. Many say, "I will never be like my father." However, by saying that to ourselves over and over we reinforce the negative. Giglio suggested we should instead say, "I'm getting to know my perfect Father in heaven more and more. I want to treat people like my Father treats people."[6] Your heavenly Father forgives people. If you want to be like Him, you must fix your gaze on Him and ask the Holy Spirit to flow forgiveness through you.

Read the following passages, and then write down what Jesus is teaching in each one.

MATTHEW 9:2-6

MATTHEW 18:21-35

LUKE 17:3-4

How might an unforgiving heart on our part block us from experiencing God's deep grace in our own lives?

REFLECT

As you think through today's lesson and Jesus' words, what feelings have His words evoked within you today?

When forgiving someone who has hurt you or hurt someone you love feels impossible, what can you do?

APPLY

What do you think the Holy Spirit is inviting you to do today?

PRAY

Lord Jesus, when I consider the lengths You went to forgive my sins, I'm in awe and I fall to my knees—giving up all the glory of heaven, becoming a baby, dealing with continual criticism, and, ultimately, going to the cross and enduring the shame and agony of the most brutal death known to man. It brings me to tears. Lord, as I bow before You and consider the price of my forgiveness, how can I do less than extend grace to those who hurt me? Yet, in my human nature, it often feels impossible. Holy Spirit, resurrect my soul. Transform me, I pray. You, Lord, are forgiving and good, and my desire is to be like You. Change me, I pray! I invite You to keep working on me and keep providing me the opportunity to follow in the footsteps of Jesus to extend forgive-ness. (Based on Eph. 4:32; Col. 3:13; Ps. 86:5.)

Now It's Your Turn

Write your own prayer in the space below.

"What He's Done," sung by Passion.[7] As you listen, allow the music to prompt your praise for the forgiveness you've received. It is my conviction that the deeper we go in internalizing our personal forgiveness, the more readily we'll extend forgiveness to others.

MEMORIZE

Review Colossians 3:13.

CHANGING OLD MESSAGES

Author Philip Yancey wrote a stirring memoir of his childhood. Raised in the fundamentalist movement in the Deep South in the '60s, Yancey was taught that people of color were cursed. From the pulpit, he was taught that God cursed Noah's son Ham, and as a result, all black people were lesser, intellectually and in other ways. Philip tells the profound story of working as an intern for the CDC and his first encounter with a professor he had admired from a distance for his brilliance. When he finally arrived at his internship in person and knocked on the door of the professor's office, the professor opened the door, and to Philip's astonishment, the professor was black. Yancey writes, "In one second, something cracks in me. . . . All summer a crisis of faith smolders inside me. *The church has clearly lied to me about race.* And about what else? Jesus? The Bible?"[8]

All of us, while growing up, received messages that were lies. For many of us, the messages we received about conflict, pain, and forgiveness were skewed. For example, I received the message that anger was wrong, and that if I was to be a "good girl," I had to keep everyone happy. That's not true. Think about it. Jesus got pretty angry in the temple and flipped a few tables, and He certainly didn't keep everyone happy. He disappointed many. I also learned that forgiveness meant exonerating someone or minimizing the pain and offering a trite response like, "That's okay." However, that's also not true. Jesus certainly didn't say to those who were crucifying Him, "That's okay!" As children we lacked the emotional ability to edit those messages. As adults, however, we must embrace the new truths of kingdom living, and part of kingdom living is handling conflict in spiritually and emotionally healthy ways.

EXPLORE

READ MATTHEW 5:38-48 AND LUKE 6:37

Fill out the chart below writing down the "Messages you've received about forgiveness" statements and "The truth about forgiveness."

MESSAGES YOU'VE RECEIVED ABOUT FORGIVENESS	THE TRUTH ABOUT FORGIVENESS

The Old Testament law was big on justice. Jesus came to *restore* justice and to give new rules for living God's way.

READ EXODUS 21:23-25 AND LEVITICUS 24:19-21

After you have finished, write a few sentences on how kingdom living is different from living under the law.

READ ROMANS 3:19-20

Why did God give the law?

REFLECT

What messages did you receive in childhood that might hinder you from embracing the truth about forgiveness?

Now that Christ has come and abolished the law through His death and resurrection, what does it mean to live in grace?

Are you a person who leans more toward justice or grace in your relationships with others?

How might either extreme damage those relationships?

APPLY

What do you feel God is inviting you to do today?

PRAY

Holy One, I realize that I received so many messages about forgiveness as a child. Some of those messages were true but some were false. Holy Spirit, help me to erase the old messages and to embrace the truth about forgiveness. Jesus, You said, "You will know the truth and the truth will set you free." I claim those words over my life, and I praise You that You invite me to walk in truth. When I am tempted to deny the pain or ease over the offense with trite phrases like, "It's okay," remind me that You continually call me to truth. When forgiveness feels impossible, remind me that You are the God who specializes in impossibilities. Help me to embrace Your heart of mercy and to offer forgiveness freely. (Based on John 8:32; Matt.19:28.)

Now It's Your Turn

Write out a prayer to the Lord inviting Him to change your heart about forgiveness.

LISTEN

"Oh the Cross," sung by Lindy Cofer (Circuit Riders Music)[9]

MEMORIZE

Review Colossians 3:13.

WHAT IS THIS THING CALLED FORGIVENESS?

My husband and I sat in a coffee shop with a well-known Christian leader. I had shared my story of abuse with him. Now I sat silently waiting for him to answer. There was a long pause. And then he said, "Becky, you must forgive." Honestly, I was a bit shocked. I remember replying, "I think I already have." He shook his head slowly and said, "I don't think so." With tears blinding my eyes, I asked, "How do you know?" He answered, "I see fear in your eyes, and if you had completely forgiven your abuser, the fear would be gone. He still holds power over you."

I asked him, "Well, what do I do?" He took several seconds to consider, then he said, "I want you to go home and ask the Holy Spirit to take you back to every memory of the abuse. In those moments, the Holy Spirit will invite you, 'Becky, will you forgive?'"

I left the coffee shop with my husband that day very conflicted. In my mind, I had forgiven. Very few people knew my story, and with those who did, I put on a brave front and said things like, "It's okay. It's over." But here's the thing, that's not forgiveness. That's denial. What I was trying to do, whether consciously or subconsciously, was numb my pain. I didn't want to feel the deep emotions of pain, betrayal, or loss. Forgiveness doesn't mean numbing our pain.

The point that Christian leader made was that I needed to go in my thinking to the place of my pain and then forgive. I realize that is the best posture for forgiveness. It ensures that we are not simply denying our pain and then offering flippant forgiveness.

Now understand, dear reader, if you've been abused, your journey of forgiveness might look different than mine. However, I do know you can't deny your pain. You must face the truth and then forgive. Only then will you find freedom from your past. And please know that I have prayed for you as I am writing this because I know forgiveness is not an easy journey!

Remember when Jesus hung on the cross? He embraced the pain, the suffering, and shame. He didn't speak from the cross, "That's okay," He cried in utter agony, "Father, forgive them, they know not what they do."

If we're going to truly forgive our debtors, as this invitation invites us to do, we need to take a deeper look at what forgiveness is and what it is not. To find the truth, we're going to dig into God's Word. Grab your Bible, and let's get started.

EXPLORE

READ MATTHEW 6:12

The Greek word for "forgive" that is used in these verses is *aphiemi*. It means "to send forth, send away." With regard to debts, it means "completely canceled."[10]

In other words, let it go. Now, let's pause for a moment and consider. There are many myths about forgiveness floating out there and I think it's important that we discern the truth. Let's look at the lies about forgiveness first, then we'll consider the truth and it's implication for our lives.

Before I go to those lies and the truth about forgiveness, I realize some hurts are bigger than others and cause more damage. For example, the abuse I experienced scarred me and left an indelible imprint on my emotional script. Forgiving that abuse was a journey. Other offenses like flippant remarks from a friend, family member, or coworker require forgiveness, but that's an easier process. Just know, dear reader, that the journey to forgive will be a part of your story, and some hurts will take longer to forgive than others.

THE LIES ABOUT FORGIVENESS

Forgiveness is dismissing or denying. When we deny our pain, we don't live in the truth. We instead try to numb our pain and act more like Buddhists than believers. Jesus came in grace and truth. *Read John 1:14. Circle the words "grace" and "truth" in your Bible.* There can be no grace without facing the truth.

Forgiveness is exonerating or excusing. Forgiveness doesn't minimize the pain the offense caused. It recognizes and feels the pain but then makes the conscious choice to let go of the desire for revenge. On the cross, Jesus felt the pain—physically, emotionally, and spiritually—as He took on the sins of the world.

Forgiveness is forgetting or ignoring. Often people say to "forgive and forget." Forgetting is actually not possible unless there's severe PTSD.[11] Even then, the memory is stored in your subconscious. *Read Hebrews 10:14–18. Circle the words "I will remember their sins no more" in your Bible.* This doesn't mean that God literally can't remember sin. If He truly forgot, He wouldn't be our all-knowing, completely sovereign God. It means He chooses to no longer dwell on our sin.

THE TRUTH ABOUT FORGIVENESS

Forgiveness is hard. It goes against our human grain. This is why Peter asked Jesus, "How many times must we forgive?" (Matt. 18:21). Honestly, if it's been easy to forgive, chances are you haven't really forgiven after all. Some offenses may have been easier to forgive than others. The truth is, you need the power of the Holy Spirit coursing through your soul to release any hurt—whether big hurts like abuse or small hurts like a rude comment from a friend. Either way, the Holy Spirit is the One who empowers us to forgive.

Forgiveness is often like peeling an onion. It often happens one layer at a time and with a whole lot of tears. Small offenses take less time; large offenses take longer. Often forgiveness is an ongoing daily choice. Please note—this does not include staying in an abusive relationship. If there is a threat of ongoing violence, forgiveness doesn't necessarily include staying in the relationship. You might need to choose in your heart to forgive again and again. Whenever you feel the pain of that hurt, you release it and send it away to the feet of Jesus.

Forgiveness doesn't benefit your offender. It sets *you* free! Often your offender might not even know they hurt you, so whatever you do, don't tell someone you've forgiven them unless they ask. Tell God, "I forgive, _____." In doing so, you are set free from the hold the other person has on you. Jesus said, "Blessed are the merciful, for they will be shown mercy" (Matt. 5:7).

Forgiveness doesn't mean staying in the relationship. If your personal safety or the safety of your children is at stake, get yourself (and your children) to a safe place and seek professional help, first for yourself.

> Forgiveness is making the conscious choice
>
> to trust God with justice.

READ MATTHEW 18:21-22

How does this story told by Jesus demonstrate the truth about forgiveness?

READ MATTHEW 18:23-35

In these verses, Jesus told a rather startling story about an unmerciful servant. In the end, the master who had forgiven the debt of the servant handed the servant over to be tortured. Then Jesus said, "This is how my heavenly Father will treat each of you unless you forgive your brother or sister from your heart" (Matt. 18:35). Ouch! The truth is, we are tortured by our own anger and desire to get even when we refuse to forgive. This is why forgiveness is such a big deal to God. As long as you don't forgive, your offender holds you captive. When you choose to forgive, you release the offender and the offense, trusting God with justice. The irony is *you* walk away free!

REFLECT

Ask the Lord to bring to mind any person you are struggling to forgive. Write the person's name below.

Write out a few sentences truthfully describing the hurt you experienced.

Then consider and answer the following questions:

What benefit have you gained from holding on to the hurt?

How has holding on to the hurt affected your outlook on life?

What would it cost you personally to forgive?

How might you understand God's grace more deeply if you chose to forgive?

What does forgiveness look like for you?

I love this prayer by author Richard Foster:

> I refuse to allow this evil to control me anymore. I will not be held in bondage to my hate any longer. But, the strength to love, is not in me. I must wait for your enabling. Now, in your great power, and with a trembling heart, I speak your word of forgiveness.[12]

APPLY

What do you feel God is inviting you to do today?

PRAY

Lord Jesus, I praise You for Your grace in my life. Because of Your great love and because You are rich in mercy, I have been forgiven through Your grace. Thank You that Your very nature is overflowing love, compassion, and grace. God, honestly, it feels impossible to continually offer forgiveness. Yet Your Word teaches me that with God all things are possible. Holy One, I renounce my own desires for revenge, and I embrace Your heart of forgiveness. Thank You that You say I am made new in Christ. The old has passed away and the new has come. Holy Spirit, I open my heart to You. I praise You that as You fill me You will forgive through me. Let grace pour through my life to others. (Based on Eph. 2:4–5; Ps. 103:8; Mark 10:27; 2 Cor. 5:17.)

Now It's Your Turn

Write a prayer expressing thanksgiving that Christ has made you new.

LISTEN

"Christ Our Hope in Life and Death," sung by Keith & Kristyn Getty[13]

MEMORIZE

Write out Colossians 3:13 from memory.

PRAYING THAT YOUR ENEMY IS BLESSED

I remember walking a beautiful beach in Southern California. As the waves gently crashed onto the shoreline, my heart was in turmoil. A group of people had hurt my husband. They had spread all sorts of lies about him. As for me, I wanted revenge. (Just keeping it real, friends!) For me, it's easier to forgive those who hurt me than those who hurt my family.

As I walked the beach, I felt the Holy Spirit not only ask, "Becky, will you forgive?" but also, "Becky, will you pray a blessing over them?" I argued, "Really, God? Do you see what they've done? What about justice? Why can't I pray like David in the Old Testament, 'Break the teeth in their mouths, O God' (Ps. 58:6)?" Now, that was a prayer I could wrap my head around! But the voice of the Holy Spirit was persistent, "I want you to pray that I bless them." Argh! Groan!

R. T. Kendall writes that we know we have forgiven when we can pray that God blesses our enemies. He wrote:

> "Total forgiveness involves an additional element:
> praying for God's blessings to rain on the lives of your offenders."[14]

It's hard to swallow that statement, isn't it? You might even feel tempted to push back. However, it is a clear biblical principle that we cannot ignore.

EXPLORE

READ JOB 2:1–13; 42:10

In case you have forgotten the story, Satan had asked God's permission to mess with Job, claiming that Job only worshiped God because God had blessed him so abundantly.

Initially, Job's friends sat empathizing in sorrow with him. However, then they began to attack Job, verbally accusing him of sin. Their theory was if God had allowed so much suffering, it had to have been because Job sinned. After Job's friends raked him over, scolding him for his supposed transgressions, God met with Job. Then God met with Job's friends and expressed His anger with them for how they treated Job. He instructed them to bring seven bulls and seven rams as an offering for a sacrifice of repentance and told them they were to go to Job humbly and ask him to pray for them (Job 42:7–8). After Job prayed for his friends, the Lord blessed Job, restoring his fortunes and giving him twice as much as he had before.

I find this story so interesting. Job could have prayed that God would punish his friends, bringing conviction and exacting justice. Instead, he prays for mercy from God on them. He blesses them. What a beautiful picture of true forgiveness!

This principle is also found in the apostle Paul's letter to the Roman church.

READ AND WRITE OUT THE WORDS OF ROMANS 12:14.

Circle the word "bless."

According to Strong's Lexicon, the word "bless" means "to confer a benefit on" or "to speak well of."[15]

How would you define the word "bless"?

The apostle Peter also understood this principle.

READ 1 PETER 3:9

Instead of revenge, we are to bow and offer blessing. This is *hard*! Praying that God blesses someone who has hurt you deeply is excruciating. That word "excruciating" is the root from which we get the word "crucifixion." When we offer forgiveness, blessing those who have hurt us, we have the opportunity to join with Jesus on the cross. Just as He offered forgiveness hanging from that cross, so we too follow His example and offer mercy and grace.

REFLECT

When you imagine blessing someone who has hurt you deeply, what comes to mind?

Ask the Lord to bring to mind someone who has hurt you or a family member. Sit in silence for a few minutes with the pain. Don't deny the pain. Embrace it. Then ask the Lord for tangible ideas to bless the person who hurt you. (Certainly, you could pray for them to be blessed. Or you might buy an anonymous gift for them.) Do you have any other ideas for how you might bless them?

How do you think it might benefit you to create a list of the ways you have experienced God's forgiveness?

In what ways has God blessed you even though you are a sinner?

APPLY

What do you feel God is speaking to you personally from this lesson?

PRAY

Holy Spirit, I praise You that You dwell within me. I ask You now to open my heart. Where there's been bitterness, uproot it. Where I am holding on to hurt, help me to let go. Where I am rehearsing the wrong done, help me to rehearse Your goodness instead. Where I am tempted to throw stones, help me to choose mercy. Lord Jesus, I long to be like You, transform me, I pray. Please continue to work in my heart in the realm of forgiveness until I am able to say by faith, "I forgive, and I choose to bless." Like Job, I will pray that those who have hurt me will be blessed by God. Thank You that I am able to trust You completely with my transformation. (Based on Heb. 12:15; Job 42:10.)

Now It's Your Turn

Write your own prayer in the space below, asking God to give you a heart of mercy and forgiveness toward others.

LISTEN

"The Blessing," sung by Kari Jobe and Cody Carnes (Elevation Worship)[16]

MEMORIZE

Review Colossians 3:13.

THE

INVITATION

TO LIVE

VICTORIOUSLY

"And Lead Us Not
into Temptation,
but Deliver Us
from the Evil One"

MATTHEW 6:13

WEEK 6 | DAY 1

WHO LEADS US INTO TEMPTATION?

As you read Jesus' words, "And lead us not into temptation," you're probably pausing. You're likely asking yourself, "Wait a minute! God doesn't lead me into temptation! What's up with this invitation?" Well, I'm glad you asked.

The Greek word *peirasmon* that's used in Matthew 6:13 "means either, temptation, trial or testing—or all three."[1] We know from James 1:13 that "when tempted, no one should say, 'God is tempting me.' For God cannot be tempted by evil, nor does he tempt anyone." However, God does lead us into trials where He allows Satan to tempt us. For example, we also know from Scripture that God allowed Job to be tested by Satan (Job 1:6–12). Jesus, too, was led into the wilderness to be tempted by Satan (Matt. 4:1–11).

Often when there are trials in our lives, the temptation to take charge or give up feels real. I remember a time in our family's life when, in the space of five months, we lost five babies. Each of our daughters and our daughter-in-law suffered miscarriages.

It was a very dark season. I remember crying out to God, "It is too much!" One Sunday in church, when each of the families was in a place of deep grief, I glanced down the row and saw all my kids with hands raised to God in surrender, worshiping the God who gives and takes away. The temptation could have been for them to shake their fist at God or even walk away from faith. Instead, they pressed in, believing that God could redeem their losses.

Times of testing always include possible temptation to give up on faith or to take matters into our own hands. Jesus handled His times of trial differently. After the Holy Spirit led Jesus into the wilderness for a time of testing, God the Father allowed Satan to tempt Jesus. Let's explore that further. Open your Bible to Matthew 4.

EXPLORE

READ MATTHEW 4:1-11

I wonder . . . when Jesus was teaching on prayer and He invited us to pray that we not be led into temptation, was He thinking about the time He spent in the wilderness? We tend to downplay the temptations that Jesus faced because He was God. However, while being fully God, He was fully human, and as such would have felt tempted like you or I would feel.

Who led Jesus into the wilderness?

Why do you think God the Spirit would lead Jesus the Son of God into the wilderness to be tempted by the devil?

When Jesus was led into the wilderness, He had been fasting for forty days. How would you describe His physical state going into the wilderness?

In the chart below, list the three ways the devil tempted Jesus and how Jesus responded.

THE TEMPTATION	JESUS' RESPONSE

Based on the way Jesus responded to temptation, what lessons can we learn about living victoriously?

Friend, we are in a battle. We live in a world where Satan is still allowed to roam freely. Jesus invites us to pray that He would protect us from temptation.

READ HEBREWS 4:14-16

What do these verses teach us about Jesus as our high priest?

Why is it important that we have a high priest who has been tempted in every area we have been tempted and yet lived without sin?

READ HEBREWS 7:25

As a result of Jesus being our sympathetic high priest, He prays for us continually, that we would not give in to temptation but that we would instead live victorious. Isn't it comforting to realize that Jesus Himself prays for us continually?

So where does temptation come from? Satan and our own lusts.

READ JAMES 1:13-14

How do our own desires lead us toward temptation?

REFLECT

When you are in a time of trial and testing and you are facing temptation, there are two practices that can be extremely helpful in your fight:

1. Quoting Scripture out loud
2. Praising God out loud

Make a battle plan. Write down the names of three worship songs you will play next time you feel tempted, as well as three Bible verses you will commit to memory to help you stand firm in the day of battle.

Though we will go through many trials and temptations in this life, remember: Jesus is victorious, and He invites you to live a life of victory in Him.

APPLY

What do you feel God is inviting you to do today?

Father God, I am so thankful that You promised that no temptation, no matter how strong, has the power to overtake me because You Yourself have provided a way of escape. Holy Spirit, search my heart. Show me where I am most often tempted. Help me as I consider Scriptures and worship songs that I can put in my arsenal to defeat the enemy. I praise You, Lord Jesus, that You are continually interceding on my behalf before the Father. I thank You that in You, I can experience victory day by day. (Based on 1 Cor. 10:13; Ps. 139:23: Heb. 7:25.)

Now It's Your Turn

Write out a prayer thanking God that the Holy Spirit will help you even in moments of temptation to stand victorious as you lean into Him.

LISTEN

"Our God Is Over All," sung by New Life Worship[2]

MEMORIZE

1 Corinthians 10:13

GROW IN SELF-AWARENESS AND KNOW YOUR PERSONAL WEAKNESSES

One of the greatest investments we can make is investing in our own self-awareness. Now, hear me. I'm not saying grow in self-obsession. So what do I mean by self-awareness?

Self-awareness is the ability to know yourself—both your strengths and your weaknesses. This is very challenging unless you ask the Holy Spirit to search your heart and give you discernment. Self-awareness includes understanding how you may be perceived by others, where you are most often tempted, and what you most often do to anesthetize pain. We all have practices we engage in to numb our pain; these might include bingeing online movies, overindulging in food or alcohol, or shopping. When you feel sad or lonely you might automatically scroll on Instagram or Amazon for hours.

Why is it important to understand ourselves? Because we need to know the weaknesses that Satan will target. Your weaknesses might not be about numbing pain, but they might be tied to your insecurities or your quest for significance. Maybe your temptation is people-pleasing and so when you're in a crowd that is gossiping, you're afraid to challenge your friends because you want them to like you. We all have weak areas, and Satan loves to target those. If we're going to live victorious Christian lives, we must grow in our self-awareness.

Jesus, as fully God, was self-aware. According to Philippians 2, He knew who He was and why He had come. As a result, He didn't have to prove Himself to anyone or grasp for power. He was completely secure in being God's beloved Son.

As humans with a sinful nature, it is much harder for us to become truly self-aware. We are experts at self-defense and, as a result, often lack awareness of our shortcomings. The psalmist David put it this way, "But who can discern their own errors? Forgive my hidden faults" (Ps. 19:12).

Today, we're going to take a deeper look at our natural tendencies, and we're going to ask the Holy Spirit to help us grow in self-awareness. Then we will be more ready when the enemy attacks. And, rest assured, he will.

EXPLORE

King Saul is the classic example of someone who was led to sin because they lacked self-awareness.

READ 1 SAMUEL 10:20–24

When Samuel had the people come forth tribe by tribe to present Saul as their king, where was Saul? How does his hiding point to his insecurity?

READ 1 SAMUEL 13:7-14

Along the way, Saul's insecurity began to drive him. He began to try to prove himself through actions not directed by God. In one instance, Saul offered up a burnt offering when Samuel was the one who was anointed to do that. Whenever we are insecure, and we don't bring that before the Lord, we end up being led into sin trying to prove ourselves.

READ 1 SAMUEL 18:1-15

Saul's insecurity led to jealous rage and ultimately to Saul attempting to murder David.

How might the story have been different if Saul had been more self-aware? What if he had honestly confessed to the Lord his crippling insecurity and asked the Lord to heal him?

As we analyze the story of King Saul, we find that because of his unresolved insecurity he:

- Ran after power and authority
- Allowed jealousy to rule his life
- Became paranoid
- Attempted murder

When we lack self-awareness, we fall more easily into temptation. Let me give you a personal example. I grew up in a rather poor ministry home where I had to wear a lot of hand-me-downs. I often felt embarrassed about my clothing. When I became a parent, I never wanted my kids to dress out of style, so without realizing my own weaknesses, I often overspent. It wasn't until a counselor pointed out that I was trying to heal the pain of my childhood by buying my kids stylish clothing that I became more self-aware. I had to then confess that to the Lord and acknowledge that He was the one who could heal my childhood pain. And, I had to learn to live on a budget.

Here's another example. Someone who had an alcoholic father may tend to over function in relationships, crossing boundaries and taking responsibility for issues that are not their own. Another person might become addicted sexually because of unresolved trauma. No matter the situation, Jesus calls us to truth and self-awareness. If you're going to live victoriously you need to know your weaknesses and learn to depend on the Holy Spirit to help you overcome those weaknesses. Whatever your weaknesses are, invite the holiness of God into that space.

This is a time to revisit the scene in the throne room that we studied in Week 2, Day 1. We are so naturally defensive that it is challenging to see our own faults. Only a deeper experience of God's holy grace can peel away the lies we tell ourselves and replace those lies with truth.

Author and Bible teacher Martyn Lloyd-Jones wrote:

> You will never make yourself feel that you are a sinner, because there is a mechanism in you as a result of sin that will always be defending you against every accusation. We are all on very good terms with ourselves, and we can always put up a good case for ourselves. Even if we try to make ourselves feel that we are sinners, we will never do it. There is only one way to know that we are sinners, and that is to have some dim, glimmering concept of God.[3]

Our self-defense mechanisms are so strong that without the Spirit of God bringing conviction, we will attempt to justify our every sin. This is why we must continually echo the prayer of David, "Search me, God, and know my heart" (Ps. 139:23).

As we spend time worshiping God in the throne room and asking Him for a deeper vision of His holiness, we discover that His forgiveness flows from His holiness right to our sin. Then we are more able to take a truthful look at the sins that lurk in our hearts. The longing of God's heart is to meet us in our weakness and cover us with His holiness.

Victory is only discovered as we realize that the heart throb of God is us. As author Dane Ortlund wrote in his book *Gentle and Lowly*, "To those who do belong to him, sins evoke holy longing, holy love, holy tenderness."[4] Even in our messiness, Christ longs for us. He understands our temptation and sympathizes with us because He has faced every temptation as we have. It is His love and mercy that lead you to repentance.

Don't be afraid to become more self-aware. Just bring your messy self to Jesus.

REFLECT

Below you will find some personal questions to answer. The more honestly you answer these questions the more you will be able to stand strong against temptation from the evil one. No one is going to check your answers. These are between you and the Holy Spirit.

When you feel bored, how do you kill time?

What would you say are your three greatest weaknesses? (While we don't want to focus on our weaknesses and spiral into shame, we need to be aware so that we can continually invite Jesus to change us.)

While we want to forget the past, we must deal with the past and bring it under the lordship of Christ or we will find ourselves repeating unhealthy patterns. If you've never done a genogram, I highly recommend it. A genogram is a visual family tree where you can list out relational patterns, as well as generational sin patterns.

Draw out your family tree, then assign symbols to represent certain patterns. For example, you might use a slanted line every time a person was cut off from another. Or you might use a circle for unplanned pregnancies. You might use a cup to represent alcoholism. The symbols should be simple figures you can draw so that when you look at your genogram you can find these generational patterns easily. Author Peter Scazzero has done an excellent job explaining this process in his book *Emotionally Healthy Discipleship.*[5]

In order to do a genogram, you would begin by asking yourself some basic questions:

How would you describe your parents, grandparents, aunts, and uncles?

How was conflict handled in your family of origin?

What are some unhealthy generational patterns that keep reoccurring? For example, in the Old Testament, Abraham lied about Sarah being his wife to protect himself. Years later, Isaac lied about his being married to Rebekah. And in the next generation, we see that Isaac and Rebekah's son Jacob was a liar. Lying was clearly passed down from one generation to the next.

Were there any occult practices or any abuse patterns? Any addictions?

Asking those questions may be challenging. However, if you don't recognize those, it's easier to repeat the patterns.

Spend some extra time with the Lord. Ask the Holy Spirit to help you leave the patterns of the past, uproot anything that has impacted you, and walk in newness of life that Jesus promised.

On a separate paper, do a genogram. (If you need a visual prompt, there are many examples of genograms on the internet.) After you've spent time filling out your genogram, write a few summary statements below.

APPLY

What do you feel God is inviting you to do in response to today's lesson?

Today take a few moments and read aloud the words of the Anglican prayer of confession:

Most merciful God,

we confess that we have sinned against you

in thought, word, and deed,

by what we have done,

and by what we have left undone.

We have not loved you with our whole heart;

we have not loved our neighbors as ourselves.

We are truly sorry and we humbly repent.

For the sake of your Son Jesus Christ,

have mercy on us and forgive us;

that we may delight in your will,

and walk in your ways,

to the glory of your Name.

Amen.[6]

Now It's Your Turn

Write your own prayer of confession in the space below.

"Abide," sung by New Life Worship[7]

Write out 1 Corinthians 10:13 on a sticky note and post it in a prominent place where you will see it often.

WEEK 6 | DAY 3

FIGHT THE ENEMY WITH THE WEAPONS GIVEN TO YOU

I have nine grandsons. They are all precious to me. It seems with boys that they are always fascinated with weapons. Sunday dinners at our house usually end up in a Nerf gun war. Our European friends say this is very "American." That's probably true. Americans seem to have a fascination with guns. I'm not sure if these toys are as popular in Europe. However, this I know, it seems little boys who don't have toy guns make their own.

In Christ's kingdom, Jesus as King was the only one who shed blood—His own. However, He calls us to be ready and prepared to fight the enemy of our soul. He gives us very specific weapons to use in our battle. Today we'll take a look at those. Open your Bible to Ephesians 6.

READ EPHESIANS 6:10–18

According to this passage, why are we to put on the full armor of God?

We are in a battle. It's not with our fellow man; it's with the evil one and his minions. The apostle Paul wrote that our struggle is not with flesh and blood. Instead, it's a spiritual battle that takes a whole lot more discernment to fight. There is a host of spiritual dark forces that are coming against us as believers. Yet we do not have to live in fear. Jesus has already won the victory. We have to understand how to put on His armor and take up the weapons He has provided.

Write out Ephesians 6:10–11. Circle the words "of God." This phrase is significant because we cannot just put on random pieces of armor. It's God's armor that we put on.

- Belt of Christ's truth
- Breastplate of Christ's righteousness
- Feet fitted with Christ's gospel
- Shield of Christ's faithfulness
- Helmet of Christ's salvation
- Sword of the Spirit—the Word of God

The imagery used here is of the armor a first-century Roman soldier would wear. The apostle Paul uses this picture to show us that we are in a battle and that we are to engage actively and aggressively, taking a stand against the schemes of the devil. And yet, the armor is completely God's provision.

Look up the following references from the Old Testament book of Isaiah. Next to each Scripture, write the correlation to the specific piece of armor mentioned in Ephesians 6.

- Isaiah 11:5
- Isaiah 49:2
- Isaiah 52:7
- Isaiah 59:17

For many years, I thought I had to try harder to put on righteousness, and I had to try harder to be faithful. Maybe you've thought that as well. But this is faulty thinking. The armor of God is about all that *God* has provided through Christ. I am clothed with *His* belt of truth, *His* righteousness, *His* gospel, *His* faithfulness, *His* salvation, and *His* sword of the Spirit. I only have to put on *His* armor.

How do I put it on? First of all, you receive His free gift of salvation. If you've never told Jesus that You receive His gift of grace, pause for a moment and tell Him that now. Second, acknowledge that Christ is your complete provision and anytime you feel tempted or feel you are under attack, shift your focus to His righteousness, His faithfulness, His gospel, and His victory. Take up the sword of the Spirit, and clobber Satan with Scripture!

READ PSALM 149:6

The psalmist gives us two very specific weapons we can use against the enemy. What are those weapons?

REFLECT

When you think of engaging in warfare, what comes to mind for you?

Two of the most common weapons the enemy uses against us are fear and discouragement. Author Susie Larson writes, "Discouragement condemns our present moment. Fear threatens our promised future."[8]

What does it mean to you personally that Christ has already accomplished your victory?

In two of the days this week, we've considered using the weapons of praying Scripture and praising God to defeat the enemy. *What does this look like in your own personal life?*

APPLY

How might God be changing your view of warfare after today's lesson? What is He inviting you to do?

PRAY

Lord Jesus, I worship You as the King of kings and the Lord of all lords. I praise You that You are my righteousness, You are my helmet of salvation, Your faithfulness covers me, and Your truth protects me. Thank You! As I at times must engage in warfare, help me not to fear the battle. Instead, I pray that I would be strong and courageous. I pray that I would stand victorious in the day of battle having clothed my heart and mind in Scripture. May I walk victorious through the power of Your Holy Spirit. (Based on Rev. 19:16; Eph. 6:14–17; Josh. 1:9.)

Now It's Your Turn

Write a prayer to the Lord based on Ephesians 6:10–18, thanking the Lord that He has covered you with His armor.

LISTEN

"Christ and Christ Crucified," sung by Lindy Cofer (Circuit Riders Music)[9]

MEMORIZE

Write out 1 Corinthians 10:13 from memory.

WEEK 6 | DAY 4

LIVING IN AUTHENTIC COMMUNITY

In the circles of Christianity I grew up in, ministry leaders were taught to not have good friends in their churches. Often that translated into no close friends at all. As a result, leaders often lived in isolation. The problem with isolation is that it often becomes a breeding ground for secret sins. Even in today's Christian circles, we have seen leaders fail morally because they weren't living in accountable and authentic community. I am more convinced than ever that each of us needs to be surrounded by a group of close friends—at least three—with whom we live transparent lives.

The apostle Paul reminded us that we were never meant to live isolated lives. He wrote, "Carry each other's burdens, and in this way you will fulfill the law of Christ" (Gal. 6:2). Part of our calling as Christ followers is to carry each other's burdens. But how can we carry each other's burdens if we aren't in close enough contact to know what those burdens are?

Today in our study we're going to look at living in authentic community and how that will benefit us in the whole area of living a victorious Christian life. What better place to start than the early church? Turn with me in your Bible to Acts 2.

EXPLORE

READ ACTS 2:42-47

When the early believers gathered, what were the four fundamentals of their time together? List them below.

The word "fellowship" that's found in verse 42 has been overused and misused in many different contexts. The Greek word for fellowship that is used here is *koinónia*. It means "sharing, partnership, participation, communion."[10] According to this definition, there really can't be fellowship where there is discord or distance in relationships.

READ ACTS 2:43-44

What was the result of the close-knit fellowship the early church enjoyed?

How often were the believers gathering?

Circle the word "together." The Greek word for "together" that's used here is *homothumadon* and means "with one mind, unanimously, with one accord."[11]

It's so interesting that in these few short verses, unity is stressed so strongly! Unity seems to be a big deal to Jesus. Hours before He was arrested in the garden, Jesus prayed that His followers would be one and that they would love one another. He prayed their community would reflect the community of the Trinity (John 17:21–23).

As I think about the church today, one of the greatest temptations we face is disunity. In the last few years, we've seen believers fight over doctrine, politics, race, and even the pandemic. We don't all have to agree, but we are one body, and we dare not hurl accusations at someone else in the body of Christ. That's Satan's job. Not ours. We are to demonstrate the love of Christ and the unity of the Trinity to the world that is watching.

READ HEBREWS 10:23-25

Community is a gift to us as believers. This is why it is so important that we do not forsake meeting together. *After reading these verses from Hebrews, why is it important that we continue gathering and embracing community?*

What do you think most often distracts believers from attending church?

REFLECT

How would you define safe, authentic community?

I firmly believe we need others in the journey who will hold us accountable. Three is a good number, as Scripture teaches that a cord of three strands is not easily broken (Eccl. 4:12).

Who are three people in your life with whom you can be completely honest?

How high of a priority is church attendance to you personally? What most often keeps you from attending?

Are you part of a safe community group with other believers? Do you feel like you can be honest in that group?

What practical ideas do you have for how you can encourage someone else in the body of Christ? List your ideas below.

APPLY

What do you feel Jesus is inviting you to do after today's study?

PRAY

Lord Jesus, I praise You that You call me your friend. Thank You also for the other friends you have brought into my life with whom I have deep fellowship. Holy Spirit, when I feel tempted, help me to be humble and honest and to ask for prayer and accountability from my friends. I realize, Lord, that in order for me to have close friends, I need to be a good safe friend for others. Help me grow my ability to offer healthy and loving friendship to others. When they open their hearts to me, help me be vigilant to keep their confidences and be intentional about not being judgmental. Help me to become known for offering empathic grace to others and one who intercedes rather than judges. (Based on John 15:15; Gal. 6:2; Matt. 7:1–3.)

Now It's Your Turn

Write a prayer to the Lord, praising and thanking Him that He is your friend and He provides a place of belonging for you.

LISTEN

"Communion," sung by Brooke Ligertwood[12]

MEMORIZE

Review 1 Corinthians 10:13.

WEEK 6 | DAY 5

STANDING IN
THE VICTORY OF
A BEAUTIFUL
BENEDICTION

Throughout church history, believers have added variations of this benediction to the end of the Lord's Prayer: "For Yours is the kingdom, the power and the glory, Amen." Many of the earliest manuscripts do not include these words, so newer translations of the Bible do not include them.

However, R. T. Kendall writes, "Many of us have prayed these beautiful words, and I myself shall continue to do so. After all, the words are absolutely true."[13]

Another great Bible teacher, Warren Wiersbe, also makes the case for this grand benediction to be added to the end of the Lord's Prayer, pointing out for us that the benediction is rooted in Scripture. Wiersbe writes:

Just because this benediction is not part of the original text doesn't mean that using it is a sin or that the benediction itself is heresy. It's generally agreed that the benediction is based on the words of David in 1 Chronicles 29 when he commissioned his son Solomon to build the temple.[14]

Let's take a deeper look. Open your Bible to 1 Chronicles 29.

EXPLORE

READ 1 CHRONICLES 29:10-13

After David announced that his son Solomon would be the one God appointed to build the temple, all the people brought their offerings of silver and gold. Then David rejoiced greatly in the Lord and praised the Lord in front of the whole assembly.

Write out David's prayer of praise in the space below.

Circle the phrase "The greatness and the power and the glory."

It is likely that the benediction that is added to the Our Father prayer was taken from this glorious expression of David's praise. The early church likely borrowed these words. They are a beautiful reminder that God's kingdom will never end and that all power and glory belong to the One to whom we pray, "Hallowed be your name."

The Our Father prayer reminds us when fear closes in around us, when the earth shakes and war breaks out, that our Father is victorious! He is to be praised eternally. The kingdom, the power, and the glory all belong to Him and Him alone.

READ ISAIAH 14:27

The Lord Almighty, our Father in heaven, cannot be thwarted. He is absolutely sovereign in power and authority. What's interesting about this verse is it follows the story of Satan who was once an angel of light, but who was filled with ambition to be greater than God (Isa. 14:12–21). As a result, Lucifer was removed from heaven.

But Isaiah 14:27 reminds us that God alone will be victorious. And because of Jesus' victory on the cross and in His resurrection, you, my friend, can be victorious as well! God's plans for your life cannot be thwarted either. You may fail from time to time. But God will offer grace and raise you back up as you submit to His authority in your life. In the end, He will accomplish all that concerns you.

READ PHILIPPIANS 1:6

How does this verse restore your hope that though Satan may accuse and discourage you, our Father will be victorious in your life through Jesus Christ?

REFLECT

It's hard to believe we are at the end of our study. I have so enjoyed writing it! It has brought such joy to my heart, and I hope to yours as well.

Reflect back over the last six weeks and answer the following questions:

How has the Our Father prayer stirred up within you a deeper understanding of our heavenly Father's love for you?

How has your heart been stirred to worship our Father for the wonder of who He is?

In what ways have you been inspired to surrender when you've considered the statement, "Your kingdom come, Your will be done, on earth as it is in heaven"?

How have you been influenced to ask audaciously for your daily bread?

How did you process the invitation to forgive?

APPLY

How will you take the Our Father prayer into your everyday life?

PRAY

Oh, my Father, You are to be worshiped and adored. I praise You that You invite me to call You "Father"! Thank You for Your ministry of healing in my life. Lord, let me echo Your words daily, "Your kingdom come, your will be done." May I walk out my life bowed before You in complete surrender. I praise You that You offer me the invitation to ask You audaciously for my daily bread. Lord, sometimes I overthink this, and I'm hesitant to ask for what I truly need. Remind me that You never tire of my persistence. You never get frustrated when I ask You audaciously for what I need. Thank You that You offer me the invitation to find freedom through forgiveness. As I have received Your forgiveness, let that forgiveness flow out of my heart to others. May I never let bitterness take root in my life. I pray, Holy Spirit, that You would remind me not to get trapped by holding grudges. Holy One, I praise You for the victory that is mine through Jesus Christ. Yours is the kingdom, the power, and glory forever and ever. Amen.

Now It's Your Turn

Write out your prayer that captures what God has done in your life through this study.

"Gloria Patri," sung by Abby Burley (New Life Worship)[15]

Recite 1 Corinthians 10:13.

In addition, since we are on the last day, take a few moments to pray the Lord's Prayer from memory.

SONG LIST

WEEK ONE

1. "Our Father," featuring Jenn Johnson, track 2 on Bethel Music, *For the Sake of the World*, Bethel Music Publishing, 2012.

2. "Run to the Father," track 1 on Cody Carnes, *Run to the Father*, Sparrow Records, 2020.

3. "How Good Is He," featuring Andi Rozier, Vertical Worship, *How Good Is He (Live)*, Essential Music Publishing, 2021.

4. "Forever & Amen," featuring Kari Jobe, track 8 on Cody Carnes, *God Is Good*, Sparrow Records, 2022.

5. "Always There," featuring Natalie Grant, track 8 on The Belonging Co, *Here (Live)*, TBCO Music, 2022.

WEEK TWO

1. "Behold Him Now," featuring Anna Byrd, track 1 on Gateway Worship, *Behold Him Now*, Gateway Create Publishing, 2022.

2. "Holy, Holy, Holy (We Bow Before Thee)," track 9 on Shane & Shane, *Hymns (Live)*, Well House Records, 2019.

3. "Endless Praise," track 6 on Charity Gayle, *Endless Praise*, Charity Gayle, 2021.

4. "A Thousand Hallelujahs," track 3 on Brooke Ligertwood, *Seven*, Sparrow Records, 2021.

5. "Jesus the Beloved," featuring Laura Hackett, track 6 on Lindy Cofer, *I Saw the Lord*, Circuit Rider Music, 2022.

WEEK THREE

1. "Simple Kingdom," featuring Cody Carnes, track 3 on Bryan & Katie Torwalt, *I've Got Good News*, Sparrow Records, 2022.

2. "Lord of It All," featuring Maggie Reed, track 14 on The Belonging Co, *See the Light (Live)*, TBCO Music, 2021.

3. "King Jesus," track 10 on Brooke Ligertwood, *Seven*, Sparrow Records, 2021.

4. "Yes (Obedience)," featuring Madison Grace Binion, track 14 on David & Nicole Binion, *Glory of Eden*, Integrity Music, 2020.

5. "Wouldn't It Be Like You," track 7 on Bryan & Katie Torwalt, *I've Got Good News*, Sparrow Records, 2022.

WEEK FOUR

1. "Honey in the Rock," featuring Brandon Lake, track 8 on Brooke Ligertwood, *Seven*, Sparrow Records, 2022.

2. "God Really Loves Us," featuring Chidima and Crowder, track 7 on Passion, *Burn Bright*, Sparrow Records, 2022.

3. "In Jesus Name (God of Possible)," on Katy Nichole, *Katy Nichole*, Centricity Music, 2022.

4. "Praise You in This Storm," track 4 on Natalie Grant, *No Stranger*, Curb Records, 2020.

5. "You Can Just Rest (Spontaneous)," featuring Jenn Johnson and Hunter Thompson, Bethel Music, *You Can Just Rest (Spontaneous)*, Bethel Music Publishing, 2018.

WEEK FIVE

1. "Jesus Paid It All," track 8 on Shane & Shane, *The Worship Initiative, Vol. 5*, Well House Records, 2014.

2. "What He's Done," track 12 on Passion, *Burn Bright*, Sparrow Records, 2022.

3. "Oh the Cross," featuring Lindy Cofer, track 2 on Circuit Rider Music, *Jesus People (Live)*, Circuit Rider Music, 2021.

4. "Christ Our Hope in Life and Death," track 1 on Keith & Kristyn Getty, *Sing! Global (Live at the Getty Music Worship Conference)*, Getty Music, 2021.

5. "The Blessing," featuring Kari Jobe and Cody Carnes, on Elevation Worship, *Graves into Gardens*, Sparrow Records, 2020.

1. "Our God Is Over All," track 3 on New Life Worship, *Over It All*, Integrity Music, 2022.

2. "Abide," track 9 on New Life Worship, *Over It All*, Integrity Music, 2022.

3. "Christ and Christ Crucified," featuring Lindy Cofer, track 1 on Circuit Riders Music, *I Saw the Lord*, Circuit Riders Music, 2022.

4. "Communion," track 4 on Brooke Ligertwood, *Seven*, Sparrow Records, 2022.

5. "Gloria Patri (Live)," featuring Abby Burley, track 6 on New Life Worship, *Over It All*, Integrity Music, 2022.

ACKNOWLEDGMENTS

My husband, Steve –

Thank you for always encouraging me to fly in my gift mix. I love how we are able to encourage each other to fully utilize our gifts of writing, speaking, and coaching! I love you tons!

My kids and kids-in-love, Bethany and Chris –

Bethany and Chris, I love how passionate you are for orphans and adoption. Your godly wisdom in raising five boys will have a ripple effect through generations. I love you both tons!

Josiah and Shaina –

Josiah, I love the way you have become the CEO of Compel Global. Watching you lead has been amazing for me. Shaina, I have loved watching you lead in the healthcare system here in Colorado! I love your hearts for prayer and the loving way you are raising your boys. I love you both tons.

Stefanie and Dave –

Stef, what a joy to watch you get your master's in social work and watch your passion for "the least" come alive. Dave, I love your heart and your passion for those who need mercy. You are both extraordinary. I love watching your kids grow up to love and follow Jesus.

Keri and Zach –

Keri, it's always a joy to watch you lead worship. It has also been wonderful watching you launch your own business, Bears Music Academy. Zach, I love your heart and passion for leadership. Both of you naturally encourage others to walk more closely with Jesus.

My grandkids!

Charlie, Ty, Joshua, Selah, Zachary, Theo, Noah, Rayna, Cayden, Kinley, Tori, Melody, Asher, and Austin! Wow! I love you guys so much and pray for each of you every day. I love watching you grow up, and I pray that each of you will follow and serve Jesus. I love you all more than you can imagine!

My agent and treasured friend, Blythe Daniel –

Blythe, you are so dear to me. In addition to being my agent, you are my dear friend. I love our times of prayer together! You are truly a prayer warrior! Love you!

All the men and women at Moody Publishers –

Judy Dunagan. Ah, in addition to being my acquisitions editor, you are my treasured friend. We have prayed for each other and for each other's kids for years. I love our times together! I am beyond blessed by our friendship! Love you.

My amazing editor, Amanda Cleary Eastep. I love your heart for detail especially when all I see is the big picture! Thank you for the hours you spend on every manuscript! You are a joy to work with!

My amazing interns –

Tiffany Curtis. Tiffany, I love working with you and am so grateful for all you do for me! Love you.

Lynsey L'Ecuyer. Lynsey, I love your heart for ministry and watching you grow in your writing and leadership. God has big plans for you! Thank you for all you do for me. Love you.

All the amazing women at New Life East! What a joy to serve and grow with you at New Life East. Love you.

NOTES

INTRODUCTION

1. Steven Croft, "Seven Reasons to Say the Lord's Prayer Each Day," Diocese of Oxford: Bishop Stephen's Blog, December 4, 2017, https://blogs.oxford .anglican.org/seven-reasons-to-say-the-lords-prayer-each-day.

2. This scanned copy was given to the author by a friend whose relatives sent it to him. There is a historic article about the poem that differs on the location of the battlefield. "Unique Poem on Lord's Prayer Found on a Battlefield," *Jefferson County Republican*, March 2, 1922, https://www.coloradohistoricnewspapers .org/?a=d&d=JCR19220302-01.2.36.

3. Lane T. Dennis, "How the Lord's Prayer Affected September 11, 2001," Crossway, September 11, 2019, https://www.crossway.org/articles/a-prayer-for-september-11/.

4. Kay Campbell, "How the Lord's Prayer Saved a 9/11 Survivor," National Catholic Reporter, September 11, 2012, https://www.ncronline.org/news/ people/how-lords-prayer-saved-911-survivor.

WEEK 1—THE INVITATION TO KNOW GOD AS FATHER

Epigraph: Anglican Church of North America, "The Lord's Prayer," in *The Book of Common Prayer* (Huntington Beach, CA: Anglican Liturgy Press, 2019), 134.

1. Barb Egan, "How Our Family Relationships Impact Us: The Father Wound," Home Alive Counselling, January 16, 2021, https://alivecounselling.com/ counselling-resources/how-our-family-relationships-impacts-us-the-father-wound/.

2. "Strong's Concordance: 5273 *hupokrités*," Bible Hub, https://biblehub.com/ greek/5273.htm.

3. "Our Father," featuring Jenn Johnson, track 2 on Bethel Music, *For the Sake of the World*, Bethel Music Publishing, 2012.

4. Timothy Keller, *Walking with God through Pain and Suffering* (New York: Penguin Books, 2013), 150. In this excerpt, Keller quotes Dan G. McCartney, *Why Does It Have to Hurt?: The Meaning of Christian Suffering* (Phillipsburg, NJ: P&R, 1998), 57–58.

5. "Run to the Father," track 1 on Cody Carnes, *Run to the Father*, Sparrow Records, 2020.

6. Kenneth E. Bailey, *The Cross & the Prodigal: Luke 15 Through the Eyes of Middle Eastern Peasants* (Downers Grove, IL: InterVarsity Press, 2005), 47.

7. "How Good Is He," featuring Andi Rozier, Vertical Worship, *How Good Is He (Live)*, Essential Music Publishing, 2021.

8. "Forever & Amen," featuring Kari Jobe, track 8 on Cody Carnes, *God Is Good*, Sparrow Records, 2022.

9. "Always There," featuring Natalie Grant, track 8 on The Belonging Co, *Here (Live)*, TBCO Music, 2022.

WEEK 2—THE INVITATION TO WORSHIP

1. Andrew Arndt, a quote from an unpublished work. Used by permission.

2. N. T. Wright, "Freedom and Framework, Spirit and Truth: Recovering Biblical Worship," *Studia Liturgica* 32, no. 2 (2002): 176–95; accessed at https://ntwrightpage.com/2016/04/05/freedom-and-framework-spirit-and-truth-recovering-biblical-worship-2/.

3. Becky Harling, *Finding Calm in Life's Chaos* (Colorado Springs: NavPress, 2005), 187.

4. John Piper, "Glorifying God . . . Period," Desiring God, July 15, 2013, https://www.desiringgod.org/messages/glorifying-god-period.

5. "Strong's Concordance: 37 *hagiazó*," Bible Hub, https://biblehub.com/greek/37.htm.

6. "Strong's Concordance: 4352 *proskuneó*," Bible Hub, https://biblehub.com/greek/4352.htm; *New Spirit Filled Life Bible, New International Version* (Nashville: Thomas Nelson, 2014), 1716.

7. A. W. Tozer, *Whatever Happened to Worship?: A Call to True Worship* (Camp Hill, PA: Christian Publications, 1985), 86.

8. "Behold Him Now," featuring Anna Byrd, track 1 on Gateway Worship, *Behold Him Now*, Gateway Create Publishing, 2022.

9. Attributed to John Francis Wade, "O Come, All Ye Faithful," Hymnary.org, https://hymnary.org/text/o_come_all_ye_faithful_joyful_and_triump.

10. Warren W. Wiersbe, *On Earth as It Is in Heaven* (Grand Rapids, MI: Baker Books, 2010), 51.

11. Becky Harling, *Who Do You Say That I Am?: A Fresh Encounter for Deeper Faith* (Chicago: Moody Publishers, 2018).

12. "Holy, Holy, Holy (We Bow Before Thee)," track 9 on Shane & Shane, *Hymns (Live)*, Well House Records, 2019.

13. George W. Knight, *The Names of God* (Uhrichsville, OH: Barbour Publishing, 2009), 131.

14. "Endless Praise," track 6 on Charity Gayle, *Endless Praise*, Charity Gayle, 2021.

15. "A Thousand Hallelujahs," track 3 on Brooke Ligertwood, *Seven*, Sparrow Records, 2021.

16. Rhonda Stoppe, "What Does It Mean to Delight Yourself in the Lord? (Psalm 37:4)," Bible Study Tools, July 14, 2019, https://www.biblestudytools.com/bible-study/topical-studies/what-does-it-mean-to-delight-yourself-in-the-lord.html.

17. "Jesus the Beloved," featuring Laura Hackett, track 6 on Lindy Cofer and Laura Hackett, *I Saw the Lord*, Circuit Rider Music, 2022.

WEEK 3—THE INVITATION TO SURRENDER

1. Candice Lucey, "Why Was the Messiah Expected to Free Israel from Rome?," Christianity.com, March 23, 2021, https://www.christianity.com/wiki/jesus-christ/why-was-the-messiah-expected-to-free-israel-from-rome.html.

2. "Simple Kingdom," featuring Cody Carnes, track 3 on Bryan & Katie Torwalt, *I've Got Good News*, Sparrow Records, 2022.

3. Timothy Keller, "Hope: Thy Kingdom Come," Gospel in Life (podcast), October 9, 2019, https://podcast.gospelinlife.com/e/hope-thy-kingdom-come/.

4. G. Campbell Morgan, *The Teaching of Christ* (Old Tappan, NJ: Revell, 1913), 219.

5. "Lord of It All," featuring Maggie Reed, track 14 on The Belonging Co, *See the Light (Live)*, TBCO Music, 2021.

6. Carolyn Arends, "The Universe in 57 Words, Seven Days Inside the Lord's Prayer," 2021, https://s3.amazonaws.com/renovareassets/downloads/The-Universe-in-57-Words-Carolyn-Arends.pdf, 28.

7. N. T. Wright, *The Lord and His Prayer* (Grand Rapids, MI: Wm. B. Eerdmans Publishing Co., 1996), 20.

8. N. T. Wright, "Look at Jesus," The Work of the People, video, 3:44, https://www.theworkofthepeople.com/look-at-jesus.

9. Robert Law, *The Tests of Life: A Study of the First Epistle of St. John* (Edinburgh: T&T Clark, 1909), 304.

10. "King Jesus," track 10 on Brooke Ligertwood, *Seven*, Sparrow Records, 2021.

11. Oswald Chambers, "March 8: The Relinquished Life," My Utmost for His Highest (website), https://utmost.org/classic/the-relinquished-life-classic/comment-page-1/.

12. Richard Foster, *Prayer: Finding the Heart's True Home* (New York: Harper Collins, 1992), 47.

13. Ibid., 54.

14. H. R. Jerajani et al., "Hematohidrosis—A Rare Clinical Phenomenon," *Indian Journal of Dermatology* 54, no. 3 (July–September 2009): 290–92, www.ncbi.nlm.nih.gov/pmc/articles/PMC2810702/.

15. Andrew Murray, *With Christ in the School of Prayer: Thoughts on Our Training for the Ministry of Intercession* (London: James Nisbet & Co., 1887), 226.

16. "Yes (Obedience)," featuring Madison Grace Binion, track 14 on David & Nicole Binion, *Glory of Eden*, Integrity Music, 2020.

17. Warren W. Wiersbe, *On Earth as It Is in Heaven* (Grand Rapids, MI: Baker Books, 2010), 77.

18. "Wouldn't It Be Like You," track 7 on Bryan & Katie Torwalt, *I've Got Good News*, Sparrow Records, 2022.

WEEK 4—THE INVITATION TO ASK AUDACIOUSLY

1. R. T. Kendall, *The Lord's Prayer* (Grand Rapids, MI: Chosen Books, 2010), 122.

2. Ibid., 118.

3. "Honey in the Rock," featuring Brandon Lake, track 8 on Brooke Ligertwood, *Seven*, Sparrow Records, 2022.

4. D. L. Moody, *Prevailing Prayer* (Chicago: Moody Publishers, 2016), 103–104.

5. Dane Ortlund, *Gentle and Lowly: The Heart of Christ for Sinners and Sufferers* (Wheaton, IL: Crossway, 2020), 79.

6. "God Really Loves Us," featuring Chidima and Crowder, track 7 on Passion, *Burn Bright*, Sparrow Records, 2022.

7. N. T. Wright, *The Lord and His Prayer* (Grand Rapids, MI: Wm. B. Eerdmans Publishing Co., 1996), 31.

8. "Strong's Concordance: 4856 *sumphóneó*," Bible Hub, https://biblehub.com/greek/4856.htm.

9. "In Jesus Name (God of Possible)," on Katy Nichole, *Katy Nichole*, Centricity Music, 2022.

10. Tony Evans, Chrystal Evans Hurst, Priscilla Shirer, Anthony Evans, and Jonathan Evans, *Divine Disruption: Holding On to Faith When Life Breaks Your Heart* (Nashville: W Publishing, 2021), 73.

11. "Unanswered Prayer—Pete Grieg," Open Doors Youth, YouTube video, 3:34, https://www.youtube.com/watch?v=lTyEo83Y0Fg.

12. "Praise You in This Storm," track 4 on Natalie Grant, *No Stranger*, Curb Records, 2020.

13. Warren W. Wiersbe, *On Earth as It Is in Heaven* (Grand Rapids, MI: Baker Books, 2010), 91.

14. Jeffrey M. Jones, "In US, 40% Get Less Than Recommended Amount of Sleep," Gallup News, December 9, 2013, https://news.gallup.com/poll/166553/less-recommended-amount-sleep.aspx.

15. "You Can Just Rest (Spontaneous)," featuring Jenn Johnson and Hunter Thompson, Bethel Music, *You Can Just Rest (Spontaneous)*, Bethel Music Publishing, 2018.

WEEK 5—THE INVITATION TO FIND FREEDOM THROUGH FORGIVENESS

1. R. T. Kendall, *The Lord's Prayer* (Grand Rapids, MI: Chosen Books, 2010), 125.

2. "Jesus Paid It All," track 8 on Shane & Shane, *The Worship Initiative, Vol. 5*, Well House Records, 2014.

3. Katie Davis, "Blood of the Father," The US Sun, May 13, 2021, https://www.the-sun.com/news/2878748/pope-shot-vatican-forgive-would-be-killer/.

4. Francis Frangipane, *Strength for the Battle* (Lake Mary, FL: Charisma House, 2017), 81.

5. Kendall, *The Lord's Prayer*, 135.

6. "Louie Giglio: Why Forgive? (LIFE Today)," originally aired January 21, 2020, YouTube video, 28:45, https://www.youtube.com/watch?v=UXpmUawrVuc.

7. "What He's Done," track 12 on Passion, *Burn Bright*, Sparrow Records, 2022.

8. Philip Yancey, *Where the Light Fell* (New York: Convergent Books, 2021), 160–61.

9. "Oh the Cross," featuring Lindy Cofer, track 2 on Circuit Rider Music, *Jesus People (Live)*, Circuit Rider Music, 2021.

10. W. E. Vine, *An Expository Dictionary of New Testament Words* (Old Tappan, NJ: Fleming H. Revell Company, 1966), 122.

11. Ruth A. Lanius and James W. Hopper, "Reexperiencing/Hyperaroused and Dissociative States in Posttraumatic Stress Disorder," *Psychiatric Times* 25, no. 13 (October 31, 2008): https://www.psychiatrictimes.com/view/reexperiencing hyperaroused-and-dissociative-states-posttraumatic-stress-disorder.

12. Richard Foster, *Prayers from the Heart* (San Francisco: HarperSanFrancisco, 1994), 17.

13. "Christ Our Hope in Life and Death," track 1 on Keith & Kristyn Getty, *Sing! Global (Live at the Getty Music Worship Conference)*, Getty Music, 2021.

14. R. T. Kendall, *Total Forgiveness* (Lake Mary, FL: Charisma House, 2007), 75.

15. "'Bless' (1757 *eneulogeo* and 2127 *eulogeo*)," Strong's Greek Lexicon, EliYah Ministries, https://www.eliyah.com/cgi-bin/strongs.cgi?file=greeklexicon &isindex=Bless.

16. "The Blessing," featuring Kari Jobe and Cody Carnes, on Elevation Worship, *Graves into Gardens, Sparrow Records, 2020.*

WEEK 6—THE INVITATION TO LIVE VICTORIOUSLY

1. R. T. Kendall, *The Lord's Prayer* (Grand Rapids, MI: Chosen Books, 2010), 145.

2. "Our God Is Over All," track 3 on New Life Worship, *Over It All*, Integrity Music, 2022.

3. Martyn Lloyd-Jones, *Seeking the Face of God: Nine Reflections on the Psalms* (Wheaton, IL: Crossway, 2005), 34.

4. Dane Ortlund, *Gentle and Lowly: The Heart of Christ for Sinners and Sufferers* (Wheaton, IL: Crossway, 2020), 70.

5. Peter Scazzero, *Emotionally Healthy Discipleship* (Grand Rapids, MI: Zondervan, 2021), 169–71.

6. Anglican Church of North America, *The Book of Common Prayer* (Huntington Beach, CA: Anglican Liturgy Press, 2019), 130.

7. "Abide," track 9 on New Life Worship, *Over It All*, Integrity Music, 2022.

8. Susie Larson, *Prevail: 365 Days of Enduring Strength from God's Word* (Bloomington, MN: Bethany House Publishers, 2020), 113.

9. "Christ and Christ Crucified," featuring Lindy Cofer, track 1 on Circuit Riders Music, *I Saw the Lord*, Circuit Riders Music, 2022.

10. "Strong's Concordance: 2842 *koinónia*," Bible Hub, https://biblehub.com/greek/2842.htm.

11. "Strong's Concordance: 3661 *homothumadon*," Bible Hub, https://biblehub.com/greek/3661.htm.

12. "Communion," track 4 on Brooke Ligertwood, *Seven*, Sparrow Records, 2022.

13. Kendall, *The Lord's Prayer*, 186.

14. Warren W. Wiersbe, *On Earth as It Is in Heaven* (Grand Rapids, MI: Baker Books, 2010), 139.

15. "Gloria Patri (Live)," featuring Abby Burley, track 6 on New Life Worship, *Over It All*, Integrity Music, 2022.

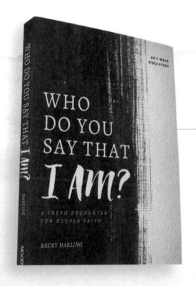
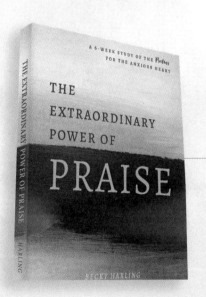

FIND DAILY PEACE
IN A WORLD OF CHAOS

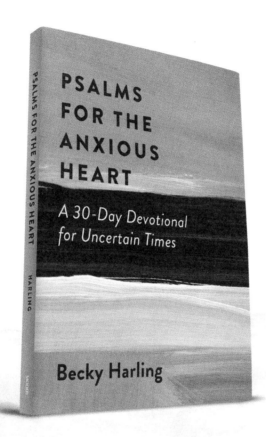

MOODY
Publishers®

From the Word to Life®

Psalms for the Anxious Heart is a short daily devotional that offers meditations of truth and peace. Each devotion includes a reading of a psalm, a brief teaching on the passage, a salient truth to cling to, and a suggested song to guide further meditation.

978-0-8024-2338-2 | also available as an eBook and audiobook

Bible Studies for Women

IN-DEPTH. CHRIST-CENTERED. REAL IMPACT.

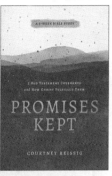

PROMISES KEPT
978-0-8024-2895-0

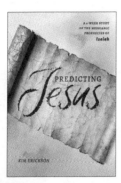

PREDICTING JESUS
978-0-8024-2511-9

AN UNEXPECTED
REVIVAL
978-0-8024-2500-3

THE GODLY KINGS OF
JUDAH
978-0-8024-2174-6

BEFORE THE THRONE
978-0-8024-2378-8

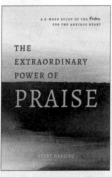

THE EXTRAORDINARY
POWER OF PRAISE
978-0-8024-2009-1

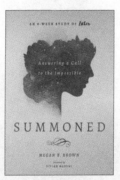

SUMMONED
978-0-8024-2169-2

A GREAT CLOUD OF
WITNESSES
978-0-8024-2107-4

Explore our Bible studies at
moodypublisherswomen.com

Also available as eBooks

MOODY PUBLISHERS
WOMEN
BIBLE STUDIES